KV-371-407

THE SPACE EXPLORER'S GALAXY GUIDE

Take a journey to the stars with this fascinating handbook of facts and fun.

Contents include:

The Expanding Universe
Mysteries in Space
Make a Simple Rocket
Who's Who in Space
Is There Life Out There?
The UFO Mystery
Make an Alien Robot
How to Make a Star Chart
Looking at the Stars
Space Dictionary
Make a Space Mobile
Will This Be the End?

Jacket illustration by Peter Gregory

The
Space Explorer's
Galaxy Guide

Jason Quark

Illustrated by Philip Emms

KNIGHT BOOKS
Hodder and Stoughton

Text copyright © Eldin Editorial Services 1979
Illustrations copyright © Hodder and Stoughton Ltd

First published in 1979 by Knight Books

The UFO Mystery and Adventures in Time and Space are
reprinted by kind permission of IPC Magazines Ltd.

Printed and bound in Great Britain for
Hodder and Stoughton Paperbacks, a
division of Hodder and Stoughton Ltd,
Mill Road, Dunton Green, Sevenoaks,
Kent (Editorial Office: 47 Bedford
Square, London, WC1 3DP) by
William Collins Sons & Co Ltd, Glasgow

ISBN 0 340 20224 6

The Expanding Universe

Today more is known about the Universe than ever before but there are still a great number of questions that remain unanswered. There are, in fact, still more questions than there are answers, and every answer that is found seems only to pose even more questions.

Distances in space are so immense it is impossible to comprehend them in everyday terms. Our galaxy is only of average size and yet if you could travel at 186,000 miles a second, the speed of light, it would take you 100,000 years to cross it. That distance in miles is six hundred quadrillion, which written in figures is, 600,000,000,000,000,000 miles! And yet our galaxy is only one in the vastness of space. Scientists have estimated that there could be something in the region of one hundred billion galaxies in the Universe.

One of the problems, when trying to imagine the immensity of the Universe, is trying to imagine such incredible distances. Perhaps the best thing you can do is to reduce the scale and in this way you will get a better understanding of the distances involved. Assume that your house is the Sun. On the same scale, the Earth will be the size of a tennis ball and the Moon the size of a ping-pong ball. From your house take one thousand steps, the largest steps you can manage, and that is where the Earth (tennis ball) should be in relation to the Sun (your house). The ping-pong ball (Moon) on the same scale will be about two and a half metres (eight feet) from the tennis ball (Earth). Now consider the fact that the distance from the Earth to the Moon is about 239,000 miles but the distance to the Sun is in the region of 93 million miles. If these distances seen remarkable, just consider that the nearest star to us is 270,000 times farther away from Earth than the Sun. When you think in terms of such distances it tends to make Man's existence rather insignificant.

It is difficult for us mere mortals to comprehend the mind-boggling vastness of space and the incredible distances between the various bodies. Using conventional rockets it takes about 2½ days to reach the Moon. Using the same speed of propulsion, and assuming such a journey is possible, it would take something like three weeks to reach the Sun, and a staggering 500,000 years to get to Proxima Centauri, the nearest star. If we wanted to continue our journey to the nearest galaxy we would be travelling for twenty thousand million years!

There are several theories as to how our universe was created. One is the *Evolutionary Theory*, which is more popularly called the *Big Bang Theory*. This states that all the matter that constitutes our Universe was once concentrated into one large lump. This lump was about the size of our present solar system but with considerable density. About twenty thousand million years ago the lump exploded to form the various bodies, including Earth, now found in space. To support this theory, scientists have pointed out the fact that all the known galaxies are moving away from each other. From this it is deducted that they must have all originated from one single point.

It has been calculated that this expansion will cease in about 25,000 million years time. When this happens, it is thought that all the matter of the Universe will then begin to move inwards until the whole system eventually collapses. Experts have predicted that this will happen in about ninety thousand million years time – so there is no need to worry about it!

The other principal theory .is known as the *Solid State Theory*. This states that the Universe as a whole had no beginning and will have no end but that it has always existed. Stars and planets within the Universe are, however, in a continual state of development. Stars are born, develop, and then die out only to be replaced by new ones, rather in the same way that all natural things develop. Part of this theory states that the amount of space between existing galaxies is expanding but all the time new material is being created within the space so that the total amount of matter within the Universe always remains the same.

In recent years many aspects of the steady state theory have been questioned and it would appear that the 'big bang' is probably closer to the truth. It must be pointed out, however, that these are purely theories based on existing knowledge and that no-one knows for certain exactly how the Universe was created.

Family Of The Sun

Early astronomers thought that the Earth was the centre of the Universe. Later they came to realise that the known planets revolve around the Sun so it was then reasoned that the Sun must be the centre. Now, however, it is realised that the Sun is just but one star in the Milky Way Galaxy. There are millions of other stars, many of which will have their own planets revolving around them.

There are nine known planets that circle the Sun. It is also possible that there is another planet beyond Pluto that has yet to be discovered. In addition to the nine principal planets, there are thousands of very small planets, called asteroids which are also circling the Sun.

The Solar System (the system of the Sun) can be regarded as being in two distinct parts – the inner planets and the outer planets. The inner planets (those closest to the Sun) – Mercury, Venus and Mars – are relatively small, whereas the outer planets (those farthest from the Sun) – Jupiter, Saturn, Uranus and Neptune – are very big. There is one odd man out and that is Pluto, the outermost planet of the known Solar System (from 1979 to 1999 Pluto will not be the outermost planet for its orbit will bring it closer to the Sun). In between the two groups of planets there are the asteroids.

The closer a planet is to the Sun the shorter the time it takes to complete its solar orbit. This period of orbit is called a year. Earth takes $365\frac{1}{4}$ days to complete its orbit. Mercury's year is only 88 Earth days, whereas a year on Pluto consists of 248 Earth years.

At the same time each planet is orbiting the Sun, it is also spinning on its axis. A complete revolution is termed a day. An earth day lasts twenty-four hours.

It is difficult to find an explanation for the creation of our Solar System within the Universe. Many theories have been put forward, but each one in turn has been found to be lacking as our knowledge increases. Some scientists have proposed the theory that our Sun once had a sister sun. These two bodies would have comprised a binary (meaning 'two') star system. Such binary stars are not uncommon. It is said that another star collided with the sister sun and that the debris resulting from this colossal collision eventually cooled down to form the planets.

It has been calculated, however, that only one star in fifty million is likely in its lifetime to hit or even come near to another star. The likelihood that the Solar System was created as the result of such a collision seems, therefore, rather remote.

Another theory regarding the creation of the Solar System suggests that a star passed close to our Sun. The gravitational pull of this star was greater than that of the Sun. This pull exerted such an influence on the Sun's gaseous content that some of it was pulled away completely.

Some of this matter was attracted to the passing star but a great deal of it was left in space. Eventually this loose material condensed into the various planets. These planets were still close enough to the Sun to be retained within its gravitational pull and so they have continued to orbit the Sun ever since.

This theory suffers from the same objection as the collision idea – the possibility of it actually happening is so remote that scientists have now largely rejected it.

Current theory suggests that the planets were formed from a cloud of gas and solid matter that used to surround the Sun. The cloud was in a state of constant change as the elements within it reacted continuously to one another. Gradually

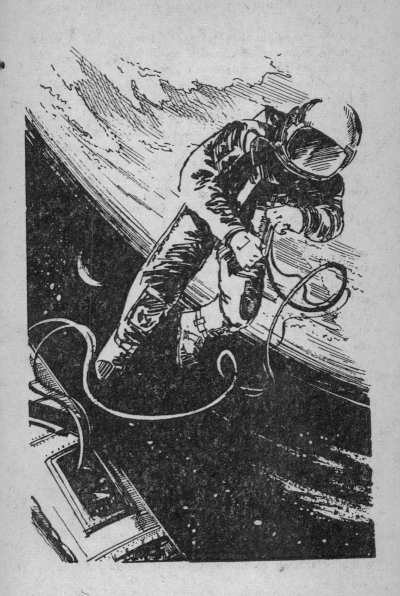

within it reacted continuously to one another. Gradually many of the gases filtered off into space and the residue material formed together into three large bodies, called protoplanets. In the course of time these protoplanets eventually broke up to form the planets that constitute the present system.

The Sun

The Sun is a star. As stars go, it is not particularly big nor particularly bright but it looks more impressive than the other stars simply because it is relatively close to us. It is important to us because we depend upon it for our existence, but it is not unique. There are many more similar solar systems within the galaxy.

The Sun is an enormous globe of gas with a diameter of 865,000 miles and is 93 million miles (149,600,000 kilometres) from Earth. Its volume is 1,303,600 times that of Earth. In view of this, it is perhaps surprising that its mass is only 332,946 times that of Earth. This is due to the fact that the material that makes up the Sun is less dense than the material of planet Earth.

Because it is so hot, the surface temperature being about 6000°C and that at the centre being in the region of twenty million degrees centigrade, it produces a great amount of energy.

Light from our Sun takes $8\frac{1}{3}$ minutes to reach us. Light from the next nearest star, Proxima Centauri, which is 25,000,000,000,000 miles away, takes four years to reach us.

It is estimated that the Sun is about 5000 million years old and that it should continue providing us with light and heat for at least another 5000 million years.

Mercury

Mercury is the planet nearest to the Sun, and because of this it is difficult to observe. It is almost impossible to see it with the naked eye and even with a telescope it is difficult because the Sun's light impedes the observation. In spite of this, the planet has been known since very early times and there are records of it being observed as far back as 264 BC. At that time it was thought there were two planets orbiting the Sun, as it was seen first on one side of the Sun and then on the other. One planet was called Mercury, and the other was named Apollo. It has since been discovered that Mercury and Apollo are in fact one and the same.

It is the smallest and the hottest of the inner planets. It has no atmosphere. During the day the temperature on the planet is extremely hot and yet at night it is bitterly cold.

Venus

Venus is the second planet in the Solar System. It is slightly smaller than Earth. In spite of the fact that it approaches Earth closer than any other planet very little is known about it due to a dense layer of cloud that conceals its surface.

When, on 22 October 1975, the Russian space probe, Venus 9, landed on the planet, it sent back pictures very different from those that the scientists had expected. Up until that time it had been thought that the surface of the planet would look like a desert, as a result of continual erosion from wind and high temperatures. But instead of sand dunes, the photographs transmitted across the 187 million miles to

Earth showed sharp rocks piled on top of one another. The high temperature was present as predicted – it was 905°F!

Because of this high temperature there can be no water on the planet, as it would immediately be vapourised into steam. And as the atmosphere of Venus consists largely of carbon dioxide and the cloud layer contains great quantities of sulphuric acid, it is unlikely that it could support any form of life.

Earth

Earth is the only planet in the Solar System that is known to support life. It is also the only planet to have vast bodies of water on its surface. The Earth's atmosphere consists mainly of nitrogen (78%) and oxygen (20%). This atmosphere extends to four miles above the surface, but the higher you go the more rarified it becomes. In theory the atmosphere extends for 22,000 miles above the surface, but in more general terms it is generally accepted that outer space begins at about one hundred miles above the Earth.

The Earth has a diameter of 7926 miles, being 81 times larger than the Moon, its only satellite. The Earth takes 23 hours, 56 minutes, and four seconds to spin once on its axis. It takes 365 days, six hours, nine minutes, and ten seconds to orbit the Sun.

Mars

Mars is 4200 miles in diameter, takes 687 days to go around the Sun and has two satellites, Phobas and Deimos, both of which are little more than small lumps of rock.

Like Earth, Mars has caps of ice at its poles. These melt in summer and the planet shows greenish patches. It was once thought that this green could be vegetation, but space probes have revealed that Mars consists of a rocky desert and no evidence of life has been found.

As there is a vast amount of water vapour in the Martian

atmosphere, there is little doubt that rivers existed on the planet at one time.

Jupiter

Jupiter is the largest planet in the Solar System having a diameter of 88,700 miles, and thirteen moons. It has the shortest rotation period of all the planets. It takes less than ten hours for this planet to spin on its axis.

In the southern hemisphere of Jupiter there appears a large red spot, called Jupiter's Eye. This red spot is some 30,000 miles long by 8000 miles wide. It seems quite likely that this is probably a concentration of some gas such as hydrogen.

If you look at Jupiter through a telescope you should be able to see the cloud belts that move across its surface. These can be seen as parallel belts, alternatively light and dark.

Saturn

Saturn is the second largest planet in the Solar System and the sixth from the Sun. It is 95 times larger than Earth, having a diameter of 74,000 miles. Saturn has ten moons, but the most prominent feature of this planet is its ring system.

There are three rings. The outermost ring is 10,000 miles wide, that in the centre is 16,000 miles wide, and the inner ring, 17,000 miles. The rings are composed of tightly-packed material, each about ten miles thick, revolving the planet. It is thought that they are the remains of what was once a moon in Saturn orbit. Between the outermost ring and the central ring there is a definite gap, reckoned to be some 1700 miles wide, known as the Cassini Division after the Italian astronomer who discovered it.

Uranus

Uranus was discovered by William Herschel in 1781. It had been seen prior to that date but previous astronomers had thought it to be a star.

The planet is 29,000 miles in diameter and takes 84 years to orbit the Sun. It has five satellites, the largest, Titania, being some 600 miles in diameter.

In 1977 it was discovered that the planet has rings. It is thought that there could be as many as six of these rings but at present no-one knows for certain.

Neptune

Neptune was one of those planets discovered through reason rather than just observing the heavens. Irregular movements of Uranus led astronomers to reason that there was another planet nearby. A search of the probable area confirmed the presence of this body, Neptune, in 1846.

It has two satellites, Triton and Nereid. The diameter of Triton is in excess of 3500 miles (much larger than our Moon), but that of Nereid is a mere two hundred miles. It is a very cold planet, with a temperature of about minus 200°C.

Pluto

Pluto is the odd man out in the outer planets because it is so much smaller than the others. It also has the most eccentric orbit of all the planets in the Solar System.

It was discovered by Clyde Tombaugh at Lowell Observatory, Arizona, USA, in 1930, but its existence had been suggested by Percival Lowell many years before that.

Pluto has a diameter of only 3600 miles and takes 248 years to orbit the Sun. Its average distance from the Sun is 3600 million miles. Although it is the most distant planet in the Solar System, it will, for the rest of this century, be closer to the Sun than Neptune.

The Moon

The Moon is a satellite of the Earth. As the Earth moves around the Sun, so does the Moon revolve around the Earth, held in its elliptical orbit by the Earth's gravitational attraction.

The average speed of the Moon's orbit is 2300 miles an hour but it moves fastest when it is closest to Earth. Even at this speed it takes 27 days and eight hours to complete its orbit. The Moon is 2160 miles in diameter, less than a quarter the diameter of Earth.

A great deal is known about the Moon from observations made by astronomers and calculations made by scientists. In recent years the unmanned lunar probes and the manned expeditions to the Moon have provided much valuable data.

The Apollo missions have proved that the Moon was created at about the same time as Earth. The oldest Moon rocks brought back to Earth for scientific analysis were about 4,200,000 years old. It seems likely that it was formed from the same gaseous matter as the Earth. Another theory is that the Moon was formed somewhere else in the Universe and got trapped in the Earth's gravitational field as it passed near by. Some people have suggested that the Moon is not a natural object but that it was made by intelligent life forms somewhere out in space! These people believe that the Moon is hollow because it is really a gigantic spaceship, the home of flying saucers, but there is no evidence to support this idea.

Although to us on Earth the Moon appears to shine, it does not emit any light on its own. What we see is a reflection of light from the Sun. The surface of the Moon is, in fact, very dark, and because of this, it reflects only seven per cent of the Sun's light that is falling on it.

There has always been a great deal of conjecture as to how

the craters on the Moon were formed. Some scientists take the view that they were formed as the result of volcanic activity. Others believe the craters were formed through the action of meteors hitting the Moon. It is more than likely that both of these factors have been responsible.

Over the page you will see a detailed chart of the Solar System showing the nine planets that revolve around the Sun, one of which is our own planet Earth.

THE SOLAR SYSTEM

name	distance from sun in kilometres (approx.)	distance from sun in miles (approx.)	diameter in kilometres	diameter in miles
Sun			1,390,000	864,000
Mercury	58,000,000	36,000,000	4,980	3,025
Venus	108,000,000	67,000,000	12,390	7,600
Earth	149,000,000	93,000,000	12,740	7,927
Mars	228,000,000	142,000,000	6,750	4,200
Jupiter	778,000,000	465,000,000	143,220	88,700
Saturn	1,430,000,000	890,000,000	120,690	75,000
Uranus	2,880,000,000	1,783,000,000	51,440	29,300
Neptune	4,494,000,000	2,793,000,000	48,880	31,200
Pluto	5,900,000,000	3,666,000,000	12,390	3,700

rotation on axis			orbit period		satellites or moons
days	hours	mins	years	days	
25	9				
59				88	
243				225	
	23	56	1		Moon
	24	37	1	322	1. Phobos
					2. Deimos
	9	50	11	318	1. Io
					2. Europa
					3. Ganymede
					4. Callisto
					5.
					6.
					7.
					8.
					9. } Unnamed
					10.
					11.
					12.
	10	14	29	168	1. Mimas
					2. Tethys
					3. Dione
					4. Rhea
					5. Titan
					6. Hyperion
					7. Iapetus
					8. Phoebe
					9. Enceladus
	10	48	84	4	1. Miranda
					2. Umbriel
					3. Ariel
					4. Titania
					5. Oberon
	14	0	164	292	1. Triton
					2. Nereid
6	9	0	249	330	

Up, Up And Away

Space travel would not have happened if it had not been for the invention of the rocket. The development of the rocket can be traced way back to the year 900 AD, when the Chinese began making them, following the invention of gunpowder. These rockets were not, of course, used for space travel, but the Chinese were using them for warfare by the thirteenth century.

The Chinese used rockets in the thirteenth century

It was not until the present century that any real advance was made in rocket design. By 1903, the Russian scientist,

Konstantin Tsiolkovsky, had outlined the basic principles for rocket powered space flight. He realised that rockets would be necessary to enable a craft to escape the Earth's gravitational pull, and that step rockets would be needed to accomplish this.

Up until this time the fuel used for all rockets had been of a solid type. Robert Goddard of America changed all that when he experimented with petrol as a rocket fuel. His work met with success in 1926, when he fired his first liquid fuelled rocket. It travelled 56 metres (184 feet). There was still a long way to go before such rockets would travel in space, but the foundations had been laid.

During the Second World War, the Germans, headed by the brilliant scientist Wernher von Braun, advanced considerably in rocket design. Their rockets were designed purely for warfare, the V2, a rocket-propelled bomb, being the most sophisticated. In 1942, at Peenemunde, the 14 metre (47 feet) rocket made its first successful flight. Wernher von Braun went to America after the war, and another group of Germans went to Russia, so both space programmes were developed from the same basic source: the German V2, which used alcohol and liquid oxygen as its propellants.

There are two basic types of rocket which are categorised according to the type of fuel they use – liquid or solid. Solid fuel rockets are not so powerful as those powered by a liquid propellant.

The amount of fuel carried in a space rocket is much greater than the combined weight of the rocket and its craft. One of the reasons why so much fuel is needed is to *carry* the fuel!

No single rocket is powerful enough to launch a satellite or a spaceship into orbit by itself. To overcome this problem, rockets are linked together in steps, or stages. As the fuel is exhausted in one rocket, it drops away and the next rocket in sequence takes over automatically. Using this method, the craft becomes lighter and faster as it travels up from the Earth.

Several other means of propelling rockets are being con-

K. Tsiolkovsky   R.H. Goddard

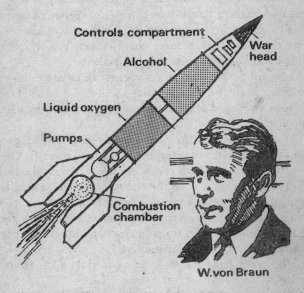

Controls compartment

War
head

Alcohol

Liquid oxygen

Pumps

Combustion
chamber

W. von Braun

German V2 and its inventor

sidered for the future. One design proposes the use of nuclear explosions to propel the rocket. Another proposal, the photon rocket, would be propelled by an intense beam of light. These rockets will be able to travel many times faster than existing rockets. Such immensely high speeds are essential if we are to travel out to the far reaches of our galaxy in our continued exploration of space.

The space age began to dawn when the first artificial satellite Sputnik 1, was put into Earth orbit on 4 October 1957. Since that time, many hundreds of satellites have been launched for a multitude of uses.

Satellites can be used for astronomy as they provide a completely different picture of the universe than that obtained on Earth, for any ground data is distorted by the Earth's atmosphere.

Communications satellites receive radio and television signals beamed from one Earth station and then amplify them before passing them on to another ground station. This has enabled the transmission of live television reports to and from many parts of the globe.

Weather satellites photograph the cloud formations above the Earth and they carry instruments that measure changes in atmospheric conditions. Such satellites also provide a useful picture of weather conditions all over the world which makes forecasting the weather for any area a great deal easier and more comprehensive than it was hitherto.

Satellites have also proved useful in improving the accuracy of maps, for photographs taken from them show a great amount of detail. Because of this wealth of detail, such satellites could also be used to spy on other countries.

Orbiting satellites are being utilised in many fields of human endeavour. They are already being used to pinpoint areas that are likely to contain oil or valuable minerals. Farmers can also use them to identify areas of disease within their fields or plantations.

Although satellites fare very well in space it is not a suitable environment for man. Anything that is in direct sunlight gets

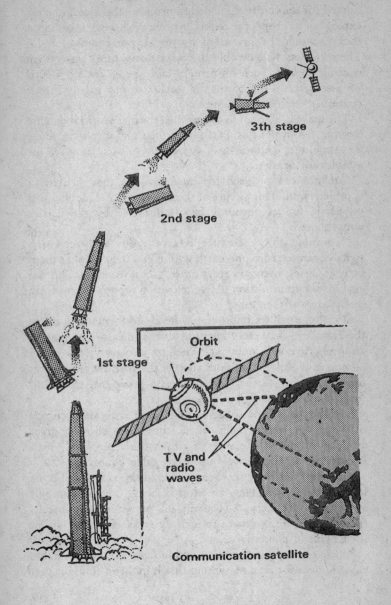

3th stage

2nd stage

1st stage

Orbit

T V and
radio
waves

Communication satellite

extremely hot, whereas if sheltered from the sun, it will be very cold.

Whenever he goes outside his spacecraft the astronaut must protect himself from the hostile features of space. To shield his eyes from the glare of the sun, his helmet is fitted with a gold-plated visor. His suit is pressurised and oxygen is supplied to him so he can breathe, for there is no air in space. An inner liquid-cooled suit controls the spaceman's body temperature. On his back he carries a large pack that contains, in addition to his air supply, his radio and an air-conditioning unit.

When travelling out into space, one of the first problems to be overcome is that of the Earth's gravity. To escape this pull, a rocket must leave the Earth at a speed in excess of 17,500 miles an hour. Once out of the Earth's atmosphere, the gravitational pull is less and there is no air to impede the craft's progress.

As there is no gravitational pull when away from a planet, objects in space have no weight. Because of this, everything, including the astronauts themselves, has to be made secure or it will float around in the spacecraft. This weightlessness can affect the bodily functions of astronauts, so great care has to be taken to ensure that anyone venturing into space is medically fit, both before and after the experience.

Eating and drinking is accomplished by having much of the food specially prepared in tubes, rather like toothpaste tubes, which are used to squeeze the food into the mouth. Sleeping is also a problem, and this has to be accomplished by securing the astronauts in sleeping bags which are fixed to the walls of the craft to prevent the astronauts from floating around.

Four short years after the launching of the first satellite, man himself travelled in space when Yuri Gagarin orbited the Earth in Vostok 1. He made only one orbit of Earth, but it paved the way for subsequent manned flights. A month after Gagarin's flight, the Americans were ready to put their first man into space. This was Commander Alan Shepard, who was launched in his Mercury capsule, Freedom 7, from pad 5 at Cape Canaveral on 5 May 1961. Fifteen minutes and 22 seconds later, the capsule landed in the Atlantic Ocean.

Shepard's flight did not actually go into orbit, but completed what is termed a sub-orbital flight at a peak altitude of 186.5 kilometres (116.5 miles). This type of flight is sometimes called a ballistic trajectory, because the flight resembles that of a bullet fired from a gun. The gun in this case was a 348,000 newton (78,000 lbs) thrust Redstone rocket, which carried the capsule up to a height of 116 miles and then ejected it. The capsule was then allowed to follow a natural curved path and fall back to Earth.

Although the Mercury capsule did not go into orbit on this occasion, it was designed to do just that. After a further sub-orbital flight, this time made by Captain Virgil 'Gus' Grissom in July 1961, America put its first man into orbit on 20 February 1962. John Glenn was the astronaut bestowed with this honour. He made three orbits and landed successfully in the Atlantic Ocean. His flight had lasted four hours and 56 minutes.

With this flight Glenn became the fifth man to be put into space. First had been Gagarin, followed by Shepard a month later. Virgil Grissom then completed a fifteen minute sub-orbital flight, to be followed by the second Russian, Herman Titov, on 6 August 1961. With John Glenn's full orbital flight, the Americans had entered the race into space.

Make A Simple Rocket

This rocket is very easy to make. All you need is an empty washing up liquid container, a length of cotton, a drinking straw, some sticky tape and a long thin balloon.

Cut the bottom off the washing up liquid container and wash it out thoroughly. Tape the drinking straw to the side of the carton. Now thread the cotton through the straw. Tie one end of the cotton to something low and the other end to something that is a little higher. You will have to experiment to discover how steep you can make the slope formed by the cotton – it depends upon the weight of the carton and the strength of the balloon.

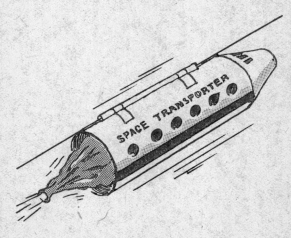

Push the balloon into the washing up liquid container and then blow it up as much as you can. Hold the neck of the balloon for a second or two. As the air rushes out of the balloon it will force the container to run up the thread. You may achieve more satisfactory results if you tie a peice of string loosely around the neck of the balloon to prevent the air from escaping too quickly.

To make the rocket look more realistic, scrape off all the printing from the container with wire wool and then paint it to look like a real rocket. You could even cut out some windows to make it look like a space ship. It is also possible to tape straws and such like onto the container to represent fuel pipes, but this only adds weight to the rocket and it may not go so well.

Man's First Venture Into Space

Man's first venture into space began at 09.07 Moscow time on 12 April 1961, when a spacecraft was launched from Tyuratum into Earth orbit. Travelling at almost 18,000 miles an hour at a height of between 118 kilometres (112.5 miles) and 327 kilometres (203 miles), the spacecraft, named Vostok (East), headed eastward around the globe with a man inside for the first time.

The man who made this historic flight was a 27 year old pilot, Major Yuri Alekseyevich Gagarin. He circled the Earth for 89 minutes and six seconds, strapped on a couch inside the four and a half ton craft.

Only twenty minutes after take-off he was over South America. 'The flight is normal. I feel well,' he reported back to his elated colleagues, who were monitoring and controlling the mission. Fifty-five minutes later, as he flew over Africa, he reported: 'I am withstanding the state of weightlessness well.'

Tension mounted in Russia as everyone waited for news of Gagarin's successful landing after his epic flight. Technicians and scientists watched their instruments intently as the craft re-entered the Earth's atmosphere, but the first to know that he had landed unharmed were two peasant women who were walking near the village of Smelovaka.

They had stopped to admire a spotted calf, when suddenly they saw a black ball suspended from red and white parachutes descend from the sky. As the black ball hurtled into the earth, throwing mud up into the air as it rolled over and over, the two women noticed that an orange and white figure had been ejected from the craft on the way down and was now floating towards them. The figure landed safely, unhitched his parachute, and walked towards the two women. They did not know whether to run or stay where they were, but as the figure approached, they could see that the orange was in fact some sort of flying suit and the white was a helmet. 'Don't be frightened,' said the stranger, 'I am Russian.' And the two women heaved a simultaneous sigh of relief.

The flight and subsequent successful landing had proved to be a magnificent moment for Gagarin, who for most of his life had dreamed of being a space pilot. He was born on 9 March 1934 on a collective farm near Smolensk. He did not go to school until he was seven years of age, but had to stop his studies almost immediately when the Germans invaded Russia in 1941. After the war, his family moved, and young Yuri went to a school just outside Moscow. Unfortunately, his parents were unable to afford his school fees for long. Yuri had to find himself a job well before his education was complete. Realising that to be a success in any field required knowledge, he got a job as a trainee foundryman at a factory in Moscow. It had its own vocational school where he could study in the evenings. His studies proved so successful that eventually he got a place in the Industrial Technical College at Saratov, a remarkable achievement for the son of a poor carpenter.

It was while he was at the college that Yuri became interested in space travel. As part of one of his physics lessons he had to prepare a paper on Tsiolkovsky, the father of Russian rocketry. It fired the young man's imagination, and he read everything he could find about Tsiolkovsky and his theories regarding the use of rocket motors for interplanetary travel. To add to his knowledge of space, Yuri also read all the science fiction stories he could find.

But it was obvious that there was no chance of his ever

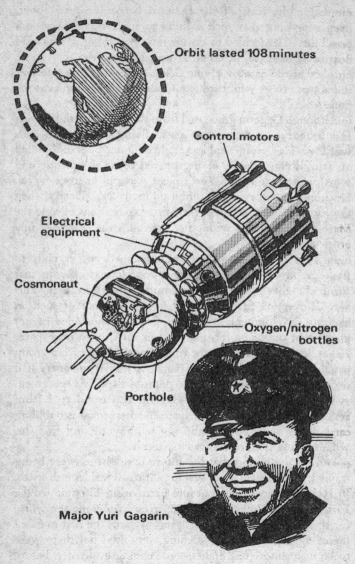

Orbit lasted 108 minutes

Control motors

Electrical
equipment

Cosmonaut

Oxygen/nitrogen
bottles

Porthole

Major Yuri Gagarin

Man's first venture into space

emulating the feats of the fictional heroes he read about, even supposing that such a thing as space travel became a possibility. He decided to do the next best thing. If he could not travel in space, he could at least get into the air – so he enrolled at the Saratov Flying School. He took flying lessons in his spare time, whilst still continuing with his studies at the college.

Although Gagarin graduated from the college with honours as a foundryman-technician, it was flying that was now his first love. He volunteered as a trainee fighter pilot and joined an army flying school. Flying proved to be an exciting and worthwhile career, but Yuri's heart was still in space travel. His hopes of achieving his ambition increased radically when the Russians began to make their first explorations beyond the Earth's atmosphere with the Sputnik, the world's first artificial satellite.

In 1959, Russia launched an unmanned rocket craft to photograph the far side of the moon. It was obvious that manned flights into space were coming closer to reality. Yuri was determined that he would not be left out of such an exciting development, and he applied to be included in any group that might be formed to train men to go into space. What he did not know at the time, was that just such a group *was* being formed, and that the Soviet space planners had decided they would use trained pilots as their first spacemen.

Within a very short time, Gagarin was transferred from his unit to begin training for space. Excitement was bubbling over inside him but he could not tell anyone, not even his wife, because the project was top secret.

During the period that the future cosmonauts were being trained, the Russians were making immense strides into space. In 1960, two dogs were put into Earth orbit. They circled the Earth eighteen times before being recovered none the worse for their fantastic journey. Progress towards the first manned flights appeared to be proceeding smoothly, but there were to be many more test flights, some ending in disaster, before Yuri Gagarin would be allowed to put on his spacesuit and step into the Vostok craft perched on top of the magnificent 38 metre high RNV (Rakyeta Nosityel Vostok) rocket.

When it did eventually take place, man's first flight into space was short compared to the flights that followed soon after. The complete flight from take-off to landing lasted for only one hour and 48 minutes; but, in addition to being the first man in space, Gagarin was also the first to have a meal in space. Obviously the meal was not absolutely necessary on such a short journey, but it had been put into the tightly-packed schedule so scientists could establish what effect the condition of weightlessness would have on eating and diges-tion.

Throughout the training period, the scientists had expressed concern regarding the effects of weightlessness upon a cosmo-naut. They were immensely relieved when it did not appear to have any effect on Gagarin's performance. Afterwards Gagarin described the sensations he experienced: 'At first it was a strange feeling,' he said, 'but I soon got used to it and could work normally. Everything was suddenly easier. I felt as if my arms and legs, in fact my entire body, no longer belonged to me. I was not sitting or lying down, I seemed to hang somewhere in the air. All unsecured objects were floating around, and when I looked at them I seemed to be dreaming. There flew the atlas, the pencil, the notebook.'

In addition to being the first man in space, Gagarin was also the first to witness with his own eyes the fact that the Earth is round. He said that the curvature of the Earth was 'quite noticeable if you looked at the horizon. And the horizon itself was incredibly beautiful. What struck me most was the dividing line between the brightly-lit Earth and the pitch-black sky, with the stars clearly visible in it – it's an incredibly narrow band, like a thin membrane surrounding the globe.'

Gagarin was given a hero's welcome on the successful com-pletion of his mission, not only in Russia but all over the world, for he opened the door to space travel. At last Man had achieved something he had dreamed of since the beginning of time. He had taken the first step in reaching for the stars. . . .

Astronauts In Training

An astronaut's training is tough and arduous. A great deal of it is concerned with the physical condition of anyone who is to venture into space, and there are daily work-outs in the gymnasium to ensure the astronaut is supremely fit. But astronauts have to have brains as well as brawn. The trainee astronaut spends a great deal of time learning about astronomy, navigation, medicine, aerodynamics, the operation of computers, meteorology, geology, and so on.

In order that the astronaut can get used to the considerable acceleration force he will have to endure, he is put into a centrifuge. This is a device that whirls the astronaut around at great speed. An even more amazing device that achieves the same objective, spins the astronaut in three different directions at the same time!

Training on the centrifuge machine will also help the astronaut combat the effects of space sickness, a nausea that is like seasickness. The first man to experience this sickness was Herman S. Titov when he orbited the Earth in Vostok 2 in August 1961. Even with the centrifuge training and the use of travel sickness pills, space nausea is still a minor problem at times.

To gain some experience of the problems that will be encountered from being weightless, the astronaut will be required to carry out certain functions in a specially adapted aircraft in which weightlessness can be simulated. Other tasks will be undertaken in a tank of water.

Because there is always the risk that something could go wrong during a mission, the astronaut will receive lessons in survival under all conditions. During this phase of the training, he will have to pass survival tests at sea, in deserts and in jungles.

During the launch of a spacecraft, the astronaut is subjected to such intense pressure that his body will feel many times heavier than normal. Once orbit is attained, all this pressure disappears, for he becomes completely weightless and can float around freely in the craft. In space there is no sound, for sound needs air to carry it. The only sounds an astronaut hears are slight noises inside the cabin and the communications he receives through his personal radio that keeps him in constant touch with the ground control.

It is, of course, essential that the astronaut is absolutely familiar with every aspect of his spaceship. It will be his home during the period of his mission, so he must know everything there is to know about it. In addition to learning the function and operation of every control in the craft and the correct interpretation of data supplied by the inboard computer and the various instruments, he must also learn exactly what procedures are to be followed in the case of an emergency: These procedures will be practised time and time again until they become second nature.

Naturally a great deal of training schedule involves practising on simulators that can reproduce conditions and events the astronaut may expect to meet in space. Everything that has to be done in space, both generally and with regard to the specific mission, is rehearsed on the ground for many long hours before the take-off.

Make Yourself
A Space Helmet

Blow up a balloon until it is a bit bigger than your head and then tie the neck to stop it going down. Put paste all over the balloon with the exception of an oval area on one side. Now stick pieces of paper all over the balloon, leaving the oval and the lower part of the balloon free of paper. Put another layer of paste on top of the paper and then stick another layer of paper on top of that. Continue this process until you have several thicknesses of paper and paste. Use white paper for the final layer.

Allow each layer to dry before adding the next. The more layers you make, the stronger will be your helmet when it is finished.

Burst the balloon and remove it from inside the paper shell and you have the basis of your space helmet. To make it look more realistic, paint it with silver or metallic paint. The easiest way to do this is to buy a can of spray paint, as used for motor cars, from your local garage.

When the paint is dry, get a sheet of polythene and stick it to the inside of the open oval. Use sticky tape for this as glue is not really suitable for the polythene. Many glues will dissolve it altogether.

Make a collar joint for the helmet by fixing a strip of silver cooking foil inside the bottom of the helmet. Use sticky tape for this. Be careful with the cooking foil or you may cut your fingers on it. Roll over the bottom of the collar so you will not cut yourself in the future.

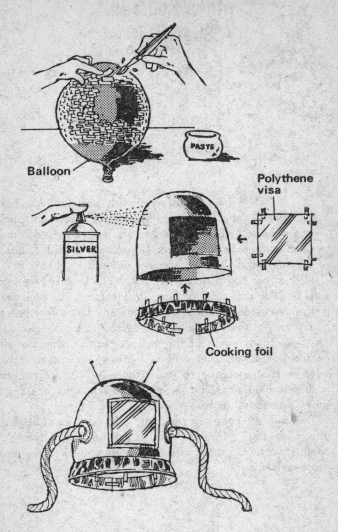

Balloon

PASTE

Polythene
visa

SILVER

Cooking foil

Now put the helmet over your head and you are ready to step out of your spacecraft, protected from the hostile environment of the planet on which you have just landed.

Make Yourself A Spacesuit

Here is a spacesuit to go with the helmet you have just made. To make the equipment look more authentic, wear a polo-necked jumper and an old pair of light-coloured trousers as the basis of your suit. If you have a padded anorak or a flying jacket this could replace the jumper.

The various components for the suit can be made from all sorts of odds and ends. On the suit illustrated, the back pack is simply a cardboard box. Strings are attached to the box to hold it on your back. Smaller boxes glued (so use old clothes!) can be used to represent the radio, special containers and control boxes. Join some of these boxes to one another with wire or rubber tubing to make them look more realistic. Rubber tubing, or thick rope, is used to represent the oxygen supply line from the back pack to the helmet.

To finish off your spacesuit, you will need an old pair of gloves, the bigger the better, and a pair of wellingtons. You could try spraying these with silver paint to make them look more realistic.

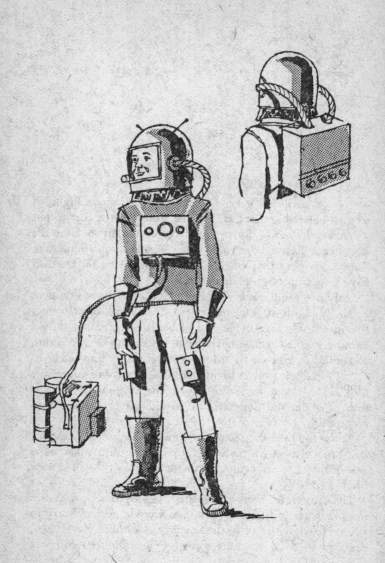

The Eagle Has Landed

After Gagarin's incredible first space flight, it seemed inevitable that the Russians would be the first to put a man on the moon. Most of the world thought so. Even the Americans believed this to be true. Wernher von Braun said, 'I am convinced that when we arrive on the moon we shall have to pass through Russian Customs.'

Only one month after Gagarin's flight, however, President Kennedy committed the Americans to the task of achieving this impossible object. He said, 'I believe this nation should commit itself to achieving the goal, before this decade is out, of landing a man on the Moon and returning him safely to Earth. No single project in this period will be more impressive to Mankind, or more important for the long-range exploration of space, and none will be so difficult or expensive to accomplish.'

At the time the President made this commitment, America had not even sent a man up into Earth orbit. What hope would they have of achieving the fantastic feat that had now been proposed?

The Americans were committed, but by this time it was becoming obvious that the Russians were in no real hurry to get to the Moon. In 1963, the Soviet leader Nikita Krushchev, declared that the Russians were not intending to compete

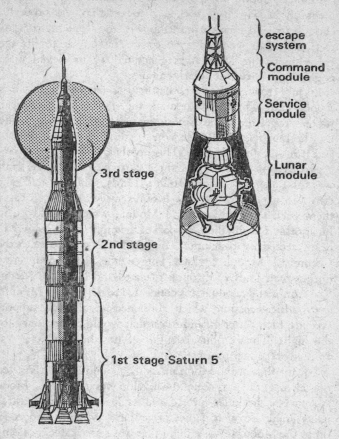

escape system

Command module

Service module

Lunar module

3rd stage

2nd stage

1st stage 'Saturn 5'

Titurn V Rocket, with detail of service and lunar modules

with the Americans on this project. Since that time the development of the two space programmes have been conducted along different lines. The Americans concentrated on the Moon, while the Russians were more concerned with the construction of unmanned probes to explore outer space, and the construction of space stations that will enable man to journey to the Moon and beyond in the future.

Kennedy's commitment ultimately resulted in the development of the Saturn V rocket, a rocket that was powerful enough to send men to the Moon. It stood 111 metres (364 feet) high and weighed 2700 tons. The power to lift the spaceship to the Moon was generated by its eleven main engines and thirty subsidiary engines.

In July 1962, two years before the launch of the first Apollo craft which was to mark the start of the American moon programme, the Americans had decided they would use the Lunar Orbit Rendezvous method of getting men to and from the lunar surface. This involved the use of a spacecraft that was composed of three parts. On top of the craft was the Lunar Excursion Module (LEM), which would take two astronauts down to the Moon's surface and then carry them back to the Command Module which would be in lunar orbit. During the early part of the flight, the LEM would be protected by panelling. The LEM was docked onto the Command Module, which housed the three man crew during their journey through space to and from the Moon. The Command Module was connected to the Service Module, a cylindrical section which contained all the life support systems, fuel, batteries, and so on that would be necessary for the flight. The combined length of the three sections was 17 metres (56 feet 6 ins).

For the first of the Moon missions, Apollo 8, the LEM was not taken, as the purpose of the mission was to orbit the Moon and survey the lunar surface. On 21 December 1968, astronauts Frank Borman, James Lovell and William Anders set off to the Moon. It was a flight that was remarkable, not only for its importance to man's conquest of space, but also because people all around the world were able to watch much of the flight on live television, as a camera was carried as part of the mission.

On Christmas Eve, the spacecraft was put into orbit around the Moon. Television pictures were transmitted back to Earth as Anders commentated on the scene that was unfolding before a breathless world. 'The colour of the soil,' he said, 'is a very whiteish grey, like a dirty beach with millions of footprints on it. Some of the craters look like somebody's been digging stiletto heels into cement and kicking up a lot of fine dust.'

In the following year came the first moon landing. After countless centuries of being confined to Earth man had at last journeyed to another world. Neil Armstrong was the American astronaut who had the unique privilege of being the first to stand on the Moon. His colleague, Edwin 'Buzz' Aldrin, followed him shortly after. The third crew member, Michael Collins, had to be content with remaining in lunar orbit in the Command Module.

The three men had lifted off from Florida on 16 July 1969. Later the same day they had fired their main engines to escape the Earth's gravity and they headed for the Moon and a permanent place in the history of space exploration.

Two days later, the whole world held its breath as the spacecraft began its orbit of the Moon and disappeared around the far side. Whilst on the far side of the Moon, radio communication with Earth was not possible. A massive sigh of relief was heaved when they eventually made their reappearance.

One of the most nail-biting moments of the whole mission came when Armstrong and Aldrin made their way into the lunar module, codenamed Eagle, separated from the command module and made their way down to the lunar surface. From Neil Armstrong came the message, 'The Eagle has wings', and everyone knew they were on their way to the most adventurous episode in man's history. People all over the world listened intently to the radio dialogue between the lunar module and mission control, as they began their descent. The dialogue itself conveys the intense excitement of the moment:

> HOUSTON: Eagle, you are go – you are go.
> Continue power descent.
> EAGLE: We've got good lock on. Altitude lights

out. And the Earth right out of our
front window.

EAGLE: 1202, 1202!

APOLLO CONTROL: Good radar data. Altitude now 33,500 feet.

EAGLE: Give us the reading on the 1202 programme alarm.

HOUSTON: We got... we're go on that alarm.

APOLLO CONTROL: Still go. Altitude 27,000 feet.

EAGLE: We throttle down better than the simulator.

APOLLO CONTROL: Altitude now 21,000 feet. Still looking very good. Velocity down now to 1200 feet per second.

HOUSTON: You're looking great to us, Eagle.

EAGLE: Good, Roger.

HOUSTON: Eagle, you're looking great . . . coming up nine minutes.

APOLLO CONTROL: We're in the approach phase, looking good. Altitude 5200 feet.

EAGLE: Manual auto altitude control is good.

APOLLO CONTROL: Altitude 4200 feet.

HOUSTON: You are go for landing. Over.

EAGLE: Roger, understand. Go for landing. 3000 feet.

EAGLE: Twelve alarm. 1201.

HOUSTON: Roger. 1201 alarm.

EAGLE: We're go. Hang tight. We're go. 2000 feet. 47 degrees.

HOUSTON: Eagle looking great. You're go.

APOLLO CONTROL: Altitude 1600 feet . . . 1400 feet.

EAGLE: 35 degrees. 750, coming down at 23. 700

The lunar module landing on the Moon

feet, 21 down. 33 degrees. 600 feet, down
at 19 . . . 540 feet . . . 400 . . . 350, down
at 4 . . . We're pegged on horizontal
velocity. 300 feet, down $3\frac{1}{2}$ a minute.
Got the shadow out there . . .

HOUSTON: Sixty seconds.

EAGLE: Lights on. Down $2\frac{1}{2}$. Forward, forward.
Good. 40 feet, down $2\frac{1}{2}$. Picking up
some dust. 30 feet, $2\frac{1}{2}$ down. Faint
shadow. Four forward. Drifting to the
right a little.

HOUSTON: Thirty seconds.

EAGLE: Drifting right. Contact light. OK,
engine stop.

HOUSTON: We copy you down, Eagle.

EAGLE: Houston, Tranquility Base here. The
Eagle has landed.

After a brief rest, the two astronauts prepared to leave the
lunar module and step foot on the moon's surface. Neil
Armstrong climbed out of the door and began his descent
down the ladder. 'I'm at the foot of the ladder. The LM foot
beds are only depressed about one or two inches, although the
surface appears to be very fine-grained as you get close to it.
It's almost like a powder. I'm going to step off now.'

As he placed his foot on the lunar surface with the words,
'That's one small step for a man, one giant leap for Mankind,'
millions of people all over the world, many of whom had
stayed up through the night to watch the event on television,
cried out with joy and elation. Man had at long last conquered
the final frontier. It had seemed absolutely impossible only a
few years earlier, and yet now the impossible was happening.
It opened up a new era for Mankind, an era that hitherto had
merely been a dream: man's conquest of space.

A short while later, Armstrong was joined on the surface
by his colleague, Buzz Aldrin. First they checked the landing
craft to make sure that everything was in working order
ready for the blast off and the reunion with the Command

Module the following day. Then they set about gathering samples of the lunar soil for subsequent analysis when they returned to Earth.

They set up experiments on the moon's surface, and then re-entered the Lunar Module for a good night's sleep. There was very little room in the Lunar Module, and to conserve what room there was, the astronauts had to pilot the craft in a standing position. In order to sleep while on the moon, they had to rig up hammocks inside the module.

For the space technicians back on Earth, the successful Moon landing was the culmination of eight years' hard work. Three men had made it to the Moon, and two of them had actually walked on the lunar surface. It was man's greatest achievement in exploration, and possibly the most dangerous, the most difficult, and undoubtedly the most exciting of *all* of man's achievements since the beginning of time.

Riding On The Moon

During the Apollo 15 mission in 1971, a most unusual vehicle was used to transport the astronauts around on the lunar surface. Called a 'Lunar Roving Vehicle' or, more popularly, the 'Moon Buggy', it looked rather like a car without a body. It was 3.10 metres (10 ft 4 ins) long, 2.06 metres (6ft 10 ins) wide, and 1.14 metres (3 ft 6 ins) high, with a weight of 480 lbs. It was designed to cope with obstacles up to 30 centimetres (12 inches) in height, could climb steep slopes with ease, and negotiate crevasses up to 70 centimetres (2 ft 4 ins) in width.

The Moon buggy was built by the Boeing company to extremely precise specifications. Rather surprisingly, the designing and building of this unique vehicle, that had to endure the vagaries of lunar conditions, took only seventeen months.

Its power source consisted of two 36 volt batteries, each of which was capable of powering the buggy on its own. But, like all aspects of space exploration, the designers believed in incorporating twice the precautionary measures that they would deem necessary on Earth. The lunar vehicle had a range of 57 miles but its missions utilised only half of its capability to ensure the safety of the astronauts.

To drive the vehicle, there was a T-shaped hand controller located on the console between the two seats, so it could be operated by either of the two astronauts. Pushing the control

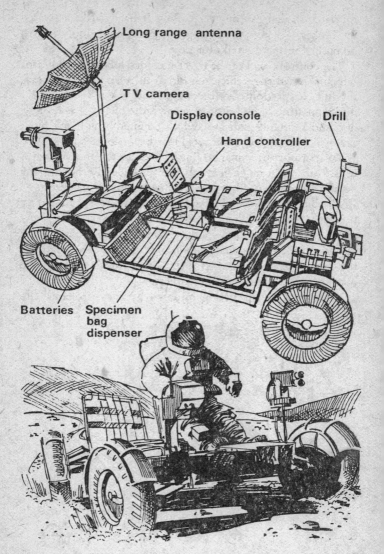

Long range antenna

T V camera

Display console

Hand controller

Drill

Batteries

Specimen bag dispenser

Lunar roving vehicle

forward, started the buggy, pulling it backwards, activated the brakes. To steer the buggy, the controller simply had to be pushed in the desired direction.

The control panel of the rover included a bearing indicator which showed the vehicle's position in relation to the lunar module, a speedometer (the rover had a top speed of 8.7 mph), an attitude indicator to show if the buggy was level or not, and a distance indicator which counted how many miles the vehicle travelled during its lunar excursions.

To transport the lunar roving vehicle to the moon, it was folded up and carried in the lunar module. Removing the vehicle from the module was a semi-automatic operation.

The buggy proved invaluable to the Apollo 15, 16 and 17 missions, for it enabled the astronauts to cover greater distances than would otherwise have been possible. Because they did not have to expend any energy in their lunar explorations, the astronauts were able to spend much more time on the moon than had been possible hitherto.

Because of the limitation imposed by the astronauts' life

The buggy was carried on the side of the lunar module

support systems, they were not permitted to drive the buggy more than three miles from the lunar module. This was a precautionary measure, designed to ensure that the two men could get back to the module in safety should the buggy break down. Three miles may not sound much, but it gave the astronauts a possible area of 28 square miles for exploration – more than twice the area they could be expected to explore if they were on foot.

The first astronauts to use the lunar roving vehicle on the moon were Dave Scott and James Irwin. During their three day stay on the lunar surface in the Apollo 15 mission, they covered a distance of $17\frac{1}{2}$ miles in the buggy.

They even enjoyed the experience of driving on the moon. As they drove along Scott enthused, 'Wow, I have never been on a ride like this before. Oh boy!' When he returned to Earth he was a little more critical, and recommended that future astronauts using similar vehicles should be strapped in. He pointed out that the moon's lack of gravity had the effect of magnifying each small bump so that the passengers were almost thrown out of their seats time after time!

A second lunar vehicle was used by John Watts Young and Charlie Duke during the Apollo 16 expedition to the Moon. They covered about fourteen miles in a lunar rover from their Descartes base. When they returned to Earth, they brought back 215 lbs of lunar material, something that would have been almost impossible without the aid of the remarkable moon buggy.

In spite of the fact that Eugene Cernan accidentally knocked a mudguard of the vehicle used in the Apollo 17 mission, the vehicle's achievements on that mission created several records. The loss of the mudguard resulted in the two astronauts being showered with moon dust when they used the buggy. After the first drive, Mission Control at Houston told Harrison Schmitt how to produce a makeshift mudguard from four of their lunar maps. Emergency lighting clips were used to attach the rather unusual mudguard to the vehicle. At the end of this last Apollo mission, the lunar roving vehicle had

Russian automatic unmanned vehicle—'Lunokhod'

covered a record 22 miles and the astronauts had collected 250 lbs of moon rock and dust for analysis.

Although the three lunar vehicles used by the Americans were a complete success, they were not the first wheeled vehicles to roam over the lunar surface. That honour goes to the Russian automatic unmanned vehicle, the lunokhod, the first of which was landed on the Sea of Rains on 17 November 1970.

The lunokhod was an automatically-controlled vehicle, brimming with sensory devices of all sorts. The principal sensor was the Rifma, an X-ray spectrometer. This was a small box positioned between the front wheels of the vehicle. It bombarded the soil beneath it with radiation, and the various materials in the lunar surface responded by emitting X-rays which were then analysed by the lunokhod's equipment. At the rear of the vehicle was a penetrometer, which dug into the lunar soil at intervals to determine the strength of the surface. This was something that had worried the Americans when they made their first moon landing, for no-one knew for certain that the moon's surface would support an astronaut or whether he would just sink into the dust!

Other equipment on the lunokhod measured radiation from the sun; and there was also a laser reflector that was used to achieve an accurate measurement of the distance between the moon and the earth. To assist the technicians on Earth to control the vehicle, it was equipped with television and telephoto cameras.

One of the problems that the operators had to overcome was the delay caused in the transmission of the television signal to Earth, and in sending orders to the vehicle. If the controllers saw the lunokhod was heading towards disaster, they had to react extremely quickly, for by the time they had received the signal and then transmitted an instruction back, it could have been too late. Luckily no such disaster occurred.

Make A Moon Base

To make this moon base you will need two washing-up liquid containers, or something similar, and an old plastic mixing bowl. If you cannot find a suitable bowl make one by pasting strips of paper over half a balloon in the same way that the space helmet was made on page 32.

Cut the two washing up cartons in half lengthways and fix them to the side of the bowl. The easiest way to do this is to use sticky tape. You now have the basic shape for your moon base, and it only has to have some windows painted on it to finish it off.

You can, if you prefer, cut out the windows and fix cellophane (coloured cellophane is very effective) to achieve a more realistic effect.

To make a lunar landscape on which you can place your moonbase use plaster of Paris or papier maché. Put jam jar and bottle tops upside down beneath the surface to provide a basis upon which you can build craters. You can paint it a greyish brown but leave the surface rather rough. It might be a good idea to scatter some small pebbles around to make the surface look authentic.

East Meets West In Space

The words 'Capriadno Was Vidit' spoken in space in 1975 heralded the dawning of a new age of space co-operation between the Russians and the Americans. The phrase, spoken by the American astronaut, Tom Stafford, to greet the Russian cosmonaut, Alexei Leonov, means 'How nice to see you again.' It was said on the occasion of the first link up in space of the Apollo and Soyuz craft, 140 miles above the Earth.

As the Apollo craft carried more fuel than the Soyuz, it was the responsibility of the Americans to perform the docking manoeuvre. Special hatches had to be made to make the docking possible. Then Tom Stafford crawled through the docking tunnel to shake hands with his Russian counterpart.

Astronaut David Slayton, who was the second man to go through the tunnel, described it as 'the world's highest sewer pipe'. One purpose of the pipe was to act as a sort of decompression chamber, because the artificial atmosphere used in the spacecraft of the two countries is different. American spacemen breathe pure oxygen in their craft, but the Russians prefer a mixture of oxygen and nitrogen. To move from one craft to the other, it was necessary for the men to spend between fifteen minutes to half an hour in the docking module while the atmosphere was changed from one system to the other. Without this change in the atmosphere and a short period to adjust to the change, the men would have

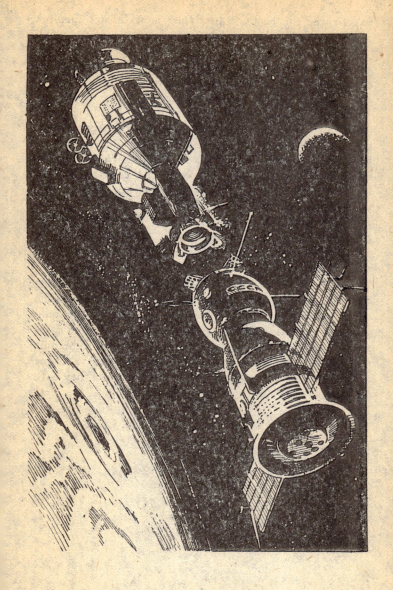

experienced the bends, a paralysing attack that sometimes affects deep sea divers.

Prior to the mission, the two crews had to get to know one another. They also had to become familiar with the other's craft. The American astronauts went to visit the Russians at Star City, the Soviet cosmonaut centre near Moscow, and the Russians visited America for training on the Apollo craft.

One of the possible problems of such a joint venture was the language barrier. To overcome this, the Russians had to learn English and the Americans Russian. To avoid mis-understandings that could still occur, each crew had to talk in the other crew's language except when speaking to their own ground controls.

The exercise was more than just a spectacular headline catcher. It had a more serious purpose. This was the carrying out of joint experiments from which both countries gained valuable knowledge.

One of the prime objectives of the mission was to devise and test a docking module that would enable the craft of each country to dock together should the need arise. This could prove of prime importance in the future, when more space stations will be constructed. It could then well become possible that one country would have to launch a rescue mission to help the spacemen of the other, should they have an accident or run into serious difficulties.

Manned Space Flights

Launch date	Mission	Crew	Duration: days: hrs: min.	Remarks
12. 4.61	Vostok 1	Gagarin	0:00:48	First manned space flight.
5. 5.61	Mercury 3	Shepard	0:00:15	First American in space (sub-orbital flight).
21. 7.61	Mercury 4	Grissom	0:00:15	Spacecraft sank (astronaut rescued).
6. 8.61	Vostok 2	Titov	:01:18	First complete day in space.
20. 2.62	Mercury 6	Glenn	0:04:55	First American in orbit.
24. 5.62	Mercury 7	Carpenter	0:04:56	Overshot landing area by 250 miles.
11. 8.62	Vostok 3	Nikolayev	3:22:22	Dual flight with Vostok 4.
12. 8.62	Vostok 4	Popovich	2:22:57	Approached within 5 km (3 miles) of Vostok 3.
3.10.62	Mercury 8	Schirra	0:09:13	Six Earth orbits.
15. 5.63	Mercury 9	Cooper	1:10:20	Twenty-two orbits. Final Mercury flight.
14. 6.63	Vostok 5	Bykovsky	4:23:06	Dual flight with Vostok 6.
16. 6.63	Vostok 6	Tereshkova	2:22:50	First woman in space.

Launch date	Mission	Crew	Duration: days: hrs: mins.	Remarks
12.10.64	Voskhod 1	Komarov Dr Yegorov Feoktistov	1:00:17	First three-man crew.
18. 3.65	Voskhod 2	Belyayev Leonov	1:02:02	First spacewalk.
23. 3.65	Gemini 3	Grissom Young	0:04:53	Changed its orbital flight; the first time this had been accomplished.
3. 6.65	Gemini 4	McDivitt White	4:01:56	First American spacewalk (20 minutes duration).
21. 8.65	Gemini 5	Cooper Conrad	7:22:56	First use of fuel cells to provide electric power.
4.12.65	Gemini 7	Bormann Lovell	13:18:35	Longest Gemini flight.
15.12.65	Gemini 6	Schirra	1:01:51	Rendezvous in space with Gemini 7 – approached to within 30 cm.
16. 3.66	Gemini 8	Armstrong Scott	0:10:42	First docking of two spacecraft.
3. 6.66	Gemini 9	Stafford Cernan	3:00:21	Cernan carried out 2 hour 7 minutes spacewalk.
18. 7.66	Gemini 10	Young Collins	2:22:47	
12. 9.66	Gemini 11	Conrad Gordon	2:23:17	
11.11.66	Gemini 12	Aldrin Lovell	3:22:34	Final Gemini mission.
23. 4.67	Soyuz 1	Komarov	1:02:45	Fatal accident when parachutes failed.
11.10.68	Apollo 7	Schirra Eisele Cunningham	10:20:11	First manned Apollo mission in Earth orbit.

Launch date	Mission	Crew	Duration: days: hrs: mins.	Remarks
26.10.68	Soyuz 3	Beregovoi	3:22:51	Rendezvous with Soyuz 2 (launched 25.10.68 – unmanned).
21.12.68	Apollo 8	Bormann Lovell Anders	6:03:00	First manned lunar orbit. Live television pictures of moon's surface transmitted to Earth.
14. 1.69	Soyuz 4	Shatalov	2:21:14	Docked with Soyuz 5.
15. 1.69	Soyuz 5	Volynov Yeliseyev Khrunov	3:00:46	Yeliseyev and Khrunov transfer to Soyuz 4.
3. 3.69	Apollo 9	McDivitt Scott Schweickart	10:01:53	First manned flight of Lunar Module.
18. 5.69	Apollo 10	Stafford Young Cernan	8:00:03	First orbit of moon by Lunar Module.
16. 7.69	Apollo 11	Armstrong Aldrin Collins	8:03:17	First manned moon landing.
11.10.69	Soyuz 6	Shonin Kubasov	4:22:42	
12.10.69	Soyuz 7	Filipchenko Volkov Gorbatko	4:22:41	
13.10.69	Soyuz 8	Shatalov Yeliseyev	4:22:41	
14.11.69	Apollo 12	Conrad Gordon Bean	10:04:36	Second moon landing. Duration of stay on surface 31 hours 31 minutes.
11. 4.70	Apollo 13	Lovell Swigert Haise	5:22:55	Mission aborted after explosion in Service Module.

Launch date	Mission	Crew	Duration: days: hrs: mins.	Remarks
1. 6.70	Soyuz 9	Nikolayev Sevastyanov	17:16:59	
31. 1.71	Apollo 14	Shepard Roosa Michell	9:00:02	Third moon landing. Duration of stay on surface 33 hours 31 minutes.
23. 4.71	Soyuz 10	Schatalov Yeliseyev Rukavishnikov	1:23:46	Docked with Salyut 1 (Russia's first space station – launched 19.4.71) but cosmonauts did not enter Salyut (possibly due to a fault or because Rukavishnikov became ill).
6. 6.71	Soyuz 11	Dobrovolski Volkov Patfayev	23:17:40	Three week stay in Salyut 1. Crew died during re-entry due to an air valve failure.
26. 7.71	Apollo 15	Scott Irwin Worden	12:07:12	First use of Lunar Roving Vehicle. Duration of stay on surface of moon 66 hours 55 minutes.
16. 4.72	Apollo 16	Young Mattingly Duke	11:01:51	Fifth Moon landing. Duration of stay on surface 71 hours 02 minutes.
7.12.72	Apollo 17	Cernan Evans Schmitt		Final Apollo mission. Duration of stay on Lunar surface 75 hours.

Launch date	Mission	Crew	Duration: days: hrs: min.	Remarks
25. 5.73	Skylab 2	Conrad Kerwin Weitz		First American manned orbiting space station (launched 14.5.73).
28. 8.73	Skylab 3	Bean Garriott Lousma		
16.11.73	Skylab 4	Carr Gibson Pogue		Completion of Skylab programme.
27. 9.73	Soyuz 12	Lazarev Makarov	2:00:00	
12.12.73	Soyuz 13	Klimuk Lebedev	8:00:00	
3. 6.74	Soyuz 14	Popovich Artyukhin	14:00:00	Occupied Salyut 3.
27. 8.74	Soyuz 15	Sarafanov Demin	2:00:00	Unsuccessful mission to Salyut 3.
3.12.74	Soyuz 16	Filipchenko Rukavishnikov	6:00:00	
11. 1.75	Soyuz 17	Gubarev Grechko	30:00:00	Mission to Salyut 4 (launched 25.12.74).
6. 4.75	Soyuz (no number)	Lazarev Makarov		Mission aborted due to malfunction of third stage rocket.
24. 5.75	Soyuz 19	Klimuk Sevastianov	63:00:00	Mission to Salyut 4.

Make A Space Station

To make an orbiting space station you will need a narrow washing up liquid container, or the cardboard tube from a roll of kitchen paper, two table tennis balls, cardboard, silver foil, and some glue.

All you have to do is glue one ball to each end of the tube you are using. To make a better and stronger join, you will find it worthwhile to glue some strips of paper inside the end of the tube first, and then glue the ball onto them. Next, you have to make a slit in each side of the tube and push a strip of cardboard through, so you have what looks like two aeroplane wings. Glue the silver foil on both sides of each wing so they become realistic-looking solar panels. Your space station is now complete, apart from painting.

You may find it easier to paint the various component parts before you put them together. If you wish to put some windows in your space station, they can also be cut out before the various components are glued together.

For added effect, why not add some radio antennae – pipe cleaners or matchsticks will serve this function quite well. Use threads to hang the model up so it looks as if it is in orbit.

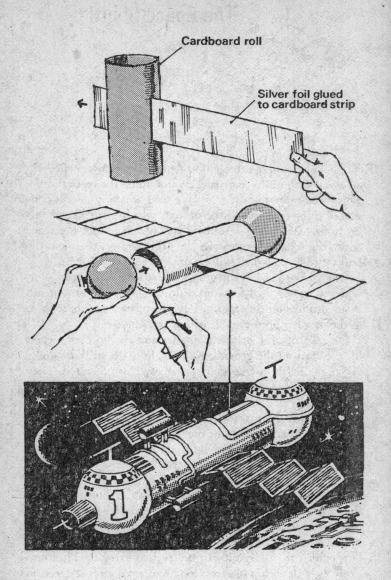

Cardboard roll

Silver foil glued to cardboard strip

The Space Shuttle

From the 1980s most American space launches will do away with multi-stage rockets and utilise the space shuttle. This looks more like an aeroplane than anything else. It consists of three main parts: the orbiter, which looks like a conventional delta wing aeroplane and which houses the space crew; the tank, which carries the orbiter into space; and the booster rockets, which will be used to launch the craft.

One of the big advantages of the space shuttle is its cost, which is lower than for conventional rockets because it can be used time and time again. Equipment used for space shots in the past has been capable of one use only.

On take off, the orbiter's engines and the booster rockets lift the craft off the ground. At a height of about thirty miles above the Earth, the booster rockets will be exhausted. They will then drop away on parachutes into the sea where they will be recovered for future use. The orbiter continues on its journey with the main fuel tank still attached until it is 120 miles from Earth. When the fuel is used up, the tank is ejected to fall back to Earth and burn up as it enters the Earth's atmosphere. Meanwhile, the shuttle will carry on into orbit at almost 18,000 miles an hour.

When its mission has been completed the shuttle re-enters the earth's atmosphere, its wings enabling it to be manoeuvred like a conventional aeroplane so it can land on a runway.

Much of the body of the shuttle itself consists of the cargo bay, which is so large it can be used to carry satellites into orbit. It is 18 metres (60 feet) long and 4.5 metres (15 feet) in diameter. Astronauts will also be able to recover satellites and bring them back to Earth for repair or dismantling.

It is designed to carry a crew of four, and up to twelve passengers in addition to its payload. Fitted out for orbiting missions of a week or more, the space shuttle will be able to perform a wide variety of tasks.

The idea for the space shuttle was born way back in the very early days of space exploration. At this time the American Air Force was already drawing up plans for a rocket-propelled spacecraft with delta wings. It was called *Dynasoar*. Due to ever-mounting costs the project never reached fruition, and the whole project was cancelled in 1963.

Although project *Dynasoar* was scrapped, a great deal of important experimental work had been carried out on the problems that would have to be solved in designing a craft suitable for use at the incredible speed encountered during its re-entry into the earth's atmosphere. In the early 1970s, the Air Force once again began working on its scheme for the space shuttle to service a manned orbiting laboratory. At this time NASA was well advanced with its Skylab programme, which consisted of an orbiting laboratory that would be serviced by modified Apollo craft. It seemed crazy for the two organisations to work on similar efforts, and so eventually it was agreed that the Air Force and NASA should work to-gether on the development of the space shuttle.

The first approach and landing test, with the shuttle fixed to the top of a Boeing 747 (Jumbo) jet, was made at the end of January, 1977, watched by 60,000 people and the television cameras of the world. The first actual flight of the shuttle took place on 12 August 1977, when it was released from the carrier jet and allowed to glide into land. It is planned that the shuttle will take its first flight in space sometime in 1979.

It is estimated that when in regular use the space shuttle will be capable of being relaunched within a week of returning from a mission. In normal conditions, however, it would be preferred to work to a fortnight turnaround time on earth to enable all the necessary checking, servicing, and launch

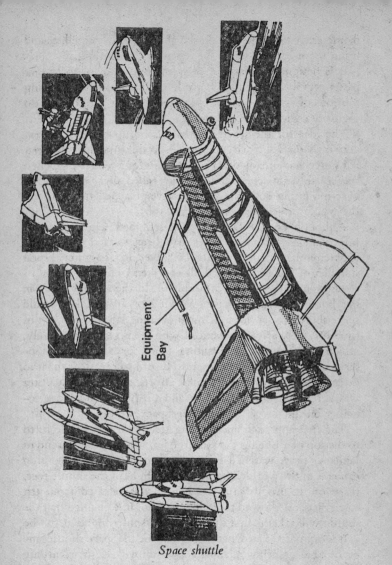

Equipment
Bay

Space shuttle

planning to be done.

Mounted near the nose of the shuttle in the upper rear of the fuselage are jets which will be used to manoeuvre the craft whilst in space.

To control the craft during landing, the shuttle has aerodynamic control surfaces similar to those of conventional aircraft. Four of these, called the elevons, which combine the effects of ordinary elevators and ailerons, are on the rear of the wings. At the bottom rear of the fuselage is another control surface which assists the elevons in controlling the pitch of the craft. It also protects the rocket engine nozzles during re-entry. Two further panels are on the rear of the vertical tail. Their function is to act as a rudder and they can also be used as a brake.

To maintain the frame of the craft at a reasonable temperature during re-entry, much of the surface of the craft is covered with special heat-resistant silica tiles. The leading edges of the craft are covered with reinforced carbon-carbon as a further protection.

Scientists from all disciplines would be the first to go up in the shuttle when it becomes operational. Among these would be doctors who could examine at first hand the effects of weightlessness and cosmic radiation on the human body, engineers to study the structure of materials in space, biochemists who could study the reactions of organic material to a space environment, astronomers who would gain a greater insight into the creation and development of the universe – the list is almost endless.

Another use for the space shuttle will be to carry crews to and from space stations. Similar craft will also be used to build the space stations in the first place.

Experimental space stations, such as Skylab and Salyut, have proved successful and have paved the way for the much larger space stations of the future.

By the end of this century it is envisaged that there will be several large space stations which will be manned permanently. Not only will such stations enable us to discover more about our universe, but they will also be essential to the longer space missions that will be accomplished in the future.

One exciting aspect of the shuttle is that it will enable

ordinary men and women to venture into space for the first time. Like the fully-trained astronauts who have preceded them, these travellers into space will have to be very fit. NASA officials have stated however that 'healthy people will be able to withstand the mild forces of acceleration and deceleration experienced'. The shuttle itself will be pressurised, so that the intrepid travellers will be able to wear ordinary clothes. The same will also be true of the space station that will be the passengers' destination, so there will be no need for large and cumbersome space suits.

In the space station artificial gravity will be maintained so there will be no need for the travellers to wear special shoes or other equipment to stop them from floating around. Food on the space station will be grown in special soil-less gardens.

Once the travellers are on the space station it will be a relatively easy step to take them on to the moon. So once the space shuttle goes into service, the possibility of taking a holiday on the lunar surface could soon become a reality.

The first people to use the shuttle will not, of course, be tourists, even though Pan American Airlines already have a long list of eager applicants. First to use the shuttle will be space scientists from Europe who will be taking up and then manning the European Spacelab. This orbiting laboratory will consist of two main parts. There will be an instrument platform open to space on which there will be telescopes, radio antennae and other measuring and observation devices. This external equipment will be controlled and monitored by the scientists inside the main part of the spacelab. This will comprise a pressurised laboratory module in which the scientists will live, carry on routine daily tasks, and conduct their experiments.

Spacelab, which will be taken up in the shuttle and brought back to Earth in the same way, will, like the shuttle itself, be reusable. This is a major departure from the procedure followed with the American Skylab and the Russian Salyut, which had to be left in space at the end of their Missions.

Who's Who In Space

ALDRIN, Edwin E.—born 20 January 1930. Second man to walk on the moon. Flew previously in Gemini 12 and did 5½ hour spacewalk. Left NASA in 1971.

ANDERS, William A.—born 17 October 1933. Lunar Module pilot on first manned flight around the moon (Apollo 8). Resigned from NASA in 1971.

N. ARMSTRONG

ARMSTRONG, Neil A.—born 5 August 1930. First man on the moon, 20 July 1969.

ARTYUHKIN, Yuri—born 1930. Cosmonaut No. 30. Flight engineer Soyuz 14.

BEAN, Alan L.—born 15 March 1932. Fourth man on the moon. Lunar Module pilot Apollo 12. Commander Skylab 3, July 1973.

BELKA—Dog passenger of Spaceship 2, launched 19 August 1960. Another dog, Strelka, was on the same mission.

BELYAYEV, Pavel I.—born 1932, died 1970. Commander Voskhod 2.

BEREGOVOI, Georgi T.—born 1921. Cosmonaut No. 12. Commander Soyuz 3.

BORMAN, Frank—born 14 March 1928. Commander Apollo 8 and Gemini 7.

BYKOVSKY, Valeri F.—born 1934. Cosmonaut No. 5. Pilot Vostok 5.

CARPENTER, M. Scott—born 1 May 1925. Made second orbital flight, Mercury 7, 24 May 1962. Left NASA in 1967.

CARR, Gerald P.—born 22 August 1932. Commander Skylab 4 in November, 1973.

CERNAN, Eugene A.—born 14 March 1934. Commander Apollo 17. The eleventh man to walk on the moon. Pilot Gemini 9. Lunar Module pilot Apollo 10.

COLLINS, Michael—born 31 October 1930. Command Module pilot Apollo 11. Pilot Gemini 10.

CONRAD, Charles—born 2 June 1930. Commander Apollo 12. The third man on the moon. Pilot Gemini 5. Commander Gemini 11. Head of Skylab project.

COOPER, L. Gordon—born 6 March 1927. Made final Mercury flight, Mercury 9. Commander Gemini 5. Retired 1970.

CUNNINGHAM, Walter—born 16 March 1932. Lunar Module pilot Apollo 7. Resigned 1971.

DEMIN, Lev—born 1926. Cosmonaut No. 32. Flight engineer Soyuz 15. The first grandfather to go into space.

DOBROVOLSKY, Georgi—born 1 June 1928. Cosmonaut No. 24. Killed during re-entry, Soyuz 11.

DUKE, Charles M.—born 3 October 1935. Lunar Module pilot Apollo 16. Tenth man on the moon.

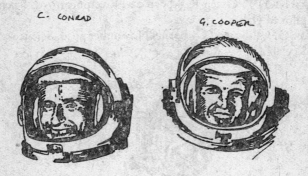

C. CONRAD   G. COOPER

EISELE, Donn F.—born 23 June 1930. Command Module pilot Apollo 7. Resigned 1972.

ENOS—Chimpanzee in Mercury 2 flight, on 29 November 1961.

EVANS, Ronald E.—born 10 November 1933. Command Module pilot Apollo 17.

FEOKTISTOV, Konstantin P.—born 1926. Cosmonaut No. 8. Scientist-cosmonaut Voskhod 1.

FILIPCHENKO, Anatoli—born 26 February 1928. Cosmonaut No. 19. Commander Soyuz 7.

GAGARIN, Yuri A.—born 9 March 1934. First man in space, Vostok 1, 12 April 1961. Killed 27 March 1968 during test flight of a military aeroplane.

GARRIOTT, Owen K.—born 22 November 1930. Science-pilot Skylab 3.

GIBSON, Edward G.—born 8 November 1936. Science-pilot Skylab 4.

GLENN, John H.—born 18 July 1921. First American in orbit, Mercury 6, 20 February 1962. Resigned 1964.

GORBATKO, Viktor—born 3 December 1934. Cosmonaut No. 21. Research engineer Soyuz 7.

GORDON, Richard F.—born 5 October 1929. Command Module pilot Apollo 12. Pilot Gemini 11. Retired 1972.

GRISSOM, Virgil I.—born 3 April 1926. Made second Mercury sub-orbital flight. Commander Gemini 3. Died in Apollo launchpad fire 27 January 1967.

HAISE, Fred W.—born 14 November 1933. Lunar Module pilot Apollo 13.

IRWIN, James B.—born 17 March 1930. Lunar Module pilot Apollo 15. Eighth man on the moon, drove Lunar Rover. Retired 1972.

KERWIN, Joseph P.—born 19 February 1932. Science-pilot Skylab 2.

KHRUNOV, Yevgeny V.—born 1933. Cosmonaut No. 15. Research engineer Soyuz 5.

KLIMUK, Pytor—born 1942. Cosmonaut No. 28. Commander Soyuz 13.

KOMAROV, Vladimir M.—born 16 March 1927. Cosmonaut No. 7. Commander Voskhod 1. Killed 23 April 1967, when re-entry parachute of Soyuz 1 snarled up.

KUBASOV, Valeri—born 7 January 1935. Cosmonaut No. 18. Flight engineer Soyuz 6. Russian Flight engineer Apollo/Soyuz.

LAIKA—The dog that became the world's first space passenger aboard Sputnik 11, launched 3 November 1957.

LAZAREV, Vasily—born 1928. Cosmonaut No. 26. Commander Soyuz 12.

LEBEDEV, Valentin—born 1942. Cosmonaut No. 29. Flight engineer Soyuz 13.

LEONOV, Alexei A.—born 30 May 1934. Cosmonaut No. 11. Made first spacewalk on 18 March 1965, Voskhod 2. Russian Commander Apollo/Soyuz.

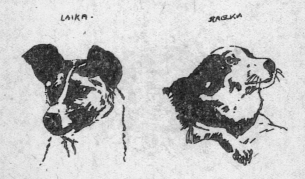

LAIKA ·   STRELKA

LOUSMA, Jack R.—born 29 February 1936. Pilot Skylab 3.

LOVELL, James A.—born 25 March 1928. Commander Apollo 13. Pilot Gemini 7. Commander Gemini 12. Command Module pilot Apollo 8.

MAKAROV, Oleg—born 1933. Cosmonaut No. 27. Flight engineer Soyuz.

MATTINGLY, Thomas K.—born 17 March 1936. Command Module pilot Apollo 16.

McDIVITT, James—born 10 June 1929. Commander Apollo 9. Commander Gemini 4.

MITCHELL, Edgar D.—born 17 September 1930. Lunar Module pilot Apollo 14. Sixth man on the moon. Retired 1972.

MUSHKA—Dog that went into space with Pchelka in Spaceship 3 on 1 December 1960.

NIKOLAYEV, Andrian G.—born 1929. Cosmonaut No. 3. Pilot Vostok 3. Commander Soyuz 9. Married Valentina Tereshkova, the first woman in space, in 1963.

PCHELKA—Dog passenger with Mushka, of Spaceship 3, launched 1 December, 1960.

POGUE, William R.—born 23 January 1930. Pilot Skylab 4.

POPOVICH, Pavel R.—born 1930. Cosmonaut No. 4. Pilot Vostok 4. Commander Soyuz 14.

P. Popovich

ROOSA, Stuart A.—born 16 August 1933. Command Module pilot Apollo 14.

RUKAVISHNIKOV, Nikolai—born 18 September 1932. Cosmonaut No. 23. Test engineer Soyuz 10.

SARAFANOV, Gennady—born 1 January 1942. Cosmonaut No. 31. Commander Soyuz 15.

SCHIRRA, Walter M.—born 12 March 1923. Commander Apollo 7. Commander Gemini 6. Retired 1969.

SCHMITT, Harrison H.—born 3 July 1935. Lunar Module pilot Apollo 17. Twelfth man on moon.

SCHWEICKART, Russell L.—born 25 October 1935. Lunar Module pilot Apollo 9.

SCOTT, David R.—born 6 June 1932. Commander Apollo 15. Seventh man on moon. Pilot Gemini 8. Command Module pilot Apollo 9.

SEVASTYANOV, Vitali—born 8 July 1935. Cosmonaut No. 22. Flight engineer Soyuz 9.

SHATALOV, Vladimir A.—born 1927. Cosmonaut No. 13. Commander Soyuz 4. Overall Commander Soyuz 8. Commander Soyuz 10.

SHEPARD, Alan B.—born 18 November 1923. First American in space, Mercury 3, 5 May 1961 (sub-orbital). Commander Apollo 14. Fifth man on the moon. Retired 1974.

SHONIN, Georgi—born 1935. Cosmonaut No. 17. Commander Soyuz 6.

STAFFORD, Thomas—born 17 September 1930. Commander Apollo 10. Pilot Gemini 6. Commander Gemini 9.

STRELKA—Dog put into space with Belka in Spaceship 2, on 19 August 1960.

SWIGERT, John—born 30 August 1931. Command Module pilot Apollo 13.

TERESHKOVA, Valentina V.—born 1937. Cosmonaut No. 6. First woman in space on 16 June 1963, Vostok 6. Married Andrian Nikolayev in 1963.

TITOV, Herman S.—born 1935. Cosmonaut No. 2. Pilot Vostok 2, the second man in orbit.

VOLKOV, Vladislav—born 23 November 1935. Cosmonaut No. 20. Flight engineer Soyuz 7. Flight engineer Soyuz 11. Killed 1971 in re-entry accident, Soyuz 11.

VOLYNOV, Boris V.—born 1934. Cosmonaut No. 14. Commander Soyuz 5.

WEITZ, Paul L.—born 25 July 1932. Pilot Skylab 2.

WHITE, Edward H.—born 14 November 1930. Pilot Gemini 4. Made first American spacewalk on 3 June 1965. Died 27 January 1967 in Apollo launchpad fire.

WORDEN, Alfred M.—born 7 February 1932. Command Module pilot Apollo 15.

YEGOROV, Boris B.—born 1937. Cosmonaut No. 9. Space doctor Voskhod 1.

YELISEYEV, Alexei S.—born 1934. Cosmonaut No. 16. Flight engineer Soyuz 5. Flight engineer Soyuz 8.

YOUNG, John W.—born 24 September 1930. Command Module pilot Apollo 10. Pilot Gemini 3. Commander Gemini 10. Commander Apollo 16.

V TERESHKOVA

Flight To The Stars

It seems impossible that man could ever travel to the stars. But it should be considered that only a few years ago a journey to the moon was regarded as pure science fiction. Not long before that, even flying was thought to be impossible. And it is not as far back as all that in history that people thought the world was flat, and that to journey across the oceans would result in your toppling off the edge of the world. Bearing all this in mind, who knows what may become possible in the years ahead?

The nearest star to Earth is Proxima Centauri, which is four and a quarter light years away. In other words, it is about 25,000,000 million miles from us. At the present level of technology it would take a spaceship something in the region of thirty thousand years to reach.

At first sight, it would appear that the only way man is likely to reach the stars would be to send a family out in a starship and hope that future generations of that family would eventually reach the stars. Another possible solution might be to deep-freeze some astronauts for thirty thousand years. But just think how out of touch the space travellers would be when they landed! Even the language spoken by the people left on Earth could have changed completely in that time. And the people on Earth would also have a higher level of civilisation by then. There would be little hope of the astronauts and the Earth people communicating with one another.

Perhaps the only feasible solution would be to have a starship manned by robots. Unfortunately, even this solution has snags, for the people on Earth could soon lose interest in any project that lasted so long.

The only real answer seems to be the development of a fuel that would enable the journey to be completed in a shorter time than is possible at present. This is, in fact, the idea that many scientists are now examining.

It is envisaged that the project, should it ever come to fruition, will involve the construction of a gigantic spaceship in space itself. This craft could be powered by a series of nuclear explosions. If enough energy could be produced, it might be possible for the ship to attain a speed of one third the speed of light. It could then cover the journey to the stars in just fifty years.

Make A Starship

Here is another space craft you can make for yourself out of materials you will find quite easily around the house.

First cut the top from a washing up liquid container. You will also need another top cut to roughly the same size. To join the two together you will also need a tube of cardboard which is rolled so it is just large enough to fit around the caps on the containers.

Glue the tube to one of the caps and then push on a disc of card, in the centre of which there is a hole just large enough to fit over the tube. To the top of this card disc glue several ping pong balls, as many as you can. Now glue the other container into the cardboard tube. When the glue is dry, paint the starship.

Next, make some small slits around the circumference of the disc and cut similar slits around the lower of the two washing up liquid cartons. These slits should only be very slight, just enough to push in some string, which is then threaded between the slits to form a reinforcing scaffolding. Glue a cone of paper to the base of the model to represent the rocket exhaust and your starship is now complete.

(*See over page for illustration.*)

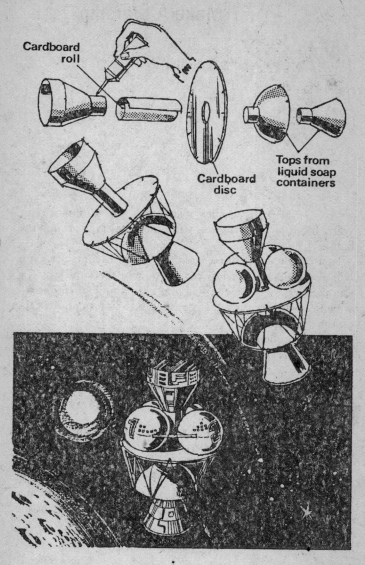

Cardboard roll

Cardboard disc

Tops from liquid soap containers

Make your own starship

Adventures In Time and Space

'When man ventures out into deep space he will encounter intelligent life,' predicts science fiction writer Arthur C. Clarke. 'The contact may be one-way, through the discovery of ruins or artifacts; it may be two-way, over radio or laser circuits; it may even be face to face. But it will occur, and it will be the most devastating event in the history of mankind.'

But if such creatures do exist, what are they like? Are they like us, or are they more like the fantastic beings dreamed up by science fiction writers? That's a question that we cannot as yet answer, so we have only the visions of fiction writers to go by. And those visions cover such a wide range of creativity that we are no nearer an answer.

Many of these fictional creatures are designed purely to frighten the reader. Some are given human characteristics but this only serves to make them even more disturbing. H. G. Wells, undisputed king of early science fiction, described the Martians in *The War of the Worlds* as possibly 'descended from beings not unlike ourselves, by a gradual development of brains and hands.'

The War Of The Worlds, possibly Wells' best known work, was originally published in serial form in 1897 and then as a book in the following year. It described the invasion of Earth by creatures from Mars. Everything that the military tries to repel the invaders fails, and it seems inevitable that the whole world will eventually be engulfed and taken over by these strange creatures. But the world is saved this awesome fate when the Martians are killed – not by sophisticated weaponry, but by common viruses to which the aliens have no resistance.

Wells was the first in the field in many areas of science fiction. If you have ever read an adventure involving man-eating plants, you can thank H. G. Wells for dreaming them up in the first place; invisible men? – yet again Wells thought of it first with *The Invisible Man*; the subject of time travel is popular with science fiction writers but it first appeared in *The Time Machine*.

One area in which Wells was not the first was space travel, for stories about journeys to the planets are as old as Mankind itself. There are many ancient legends concerning gods flying through space and time. Almost two thousand years ago, the Greek storyteller, Lucian of Samosata, described in his *True History* how high winds and a gigantic waterspout carried a Greek ship to the Moon. Much to the travellers' surprise they find that not only is the Moon inhabited but that there is a war in progress between the king of the Moon and the king of the Sun over the disputed colonisation of Jupiter.

To the purist, however, such stories are not regarded as true science fiction. In fact, there is considerable argument over the exact definition of the term 'science fiction'. Such literature used to be called by the tongue-twisting name of 'scientific-tion', but this was changed to the more straight-forward 'science fiction' in the 1920s. But what is science fiction? That is where the experts disagree. Many assert that all true science fiction was written before 1935, for in the 1930s magazines such as *Weird Tales*, *Astounding Stories* and *Amazing Stories* had set the theme and made this type of story popular. For others, the highspot of science fiction history was the 1950s, when space travel was the recurrent theme and the adventures of Dan Dare in the comic *Eagle* was required reading for all fans. When, in the late fifties and early sixties, space travel became a reality, science fiction itself had to change, and this is where the truth about the definition of science fiction can be discovered. Fans of the genre are unable to agree on an all embracing definition, for there is none.

To most people, science fiction means adventures in space and time, and what was once called tales of 'bug-eyed monsters for bug-eyed readers'. One of the earliest writers of this type of story was Jules Verne, and his works remain popular to this day. Verne, originally a playwright, produced some of the all-time classics, such as *Twenty Thousand Leagues Under the Sea*, *Journey to the Centre of the Earth*, *Around the World in Eighty Days* and *From the Earth to the Moon*.

As the twentieth century dawned, Verne and Wells were the leading science fiction writers. Nowadays they are considered old-fashioned, as technology has progressed further forward than either of them in their wildest dreams could ever have envisaged. The present-day writer of science fiction has himself to be more knowledgeable and more technically accurate if his works are to be acceptable to the general public. Because of this accent on technology, a great deal of science fiction no longer has space travel as the dominant theme.

One writer who has managed to keep up with technology, and who in many instances has been way ahead of it, is Arthur C. Clarke. His interest in science fiction was born when, as a 13-year-old schoolboy, he found some copies of *Amazing Stories* and *Astounding Stories*. From that moment he devoured every science fiction story he could find, and he even wrote some of his own, which were published in his school magazine. When he left school he joined a small group of enthusiasts who called themselves the British Interplanetary Society. The members, with Clarke's help, designed a spacecraft to carry men to the moon. At the time everyone scoffed at such a ridiculous idea, but subsequent events proved that Clarke and his colleagues were on the right track with their design.

Soon after the Second World War, Arthur C. Clarke published an article in *Wireless World* showing how Earth satellites could act as relay stations for radio and television signals. Again the reaction was sceptical, but once again Clarke was to be proved right eventually, as many such satellites now orbit the Earth. Clarke's predictions for the future include the use of animals as human servants working in the home and in factories, a dramatic drop in the world's population, and the advent of microbiological conversion of protein in petroleum products as our major source of food.

Ever since 1950, when he published *Interplanetary Flight*, Arthur C. Clarke has been at the forefront in the writing of both science fiction and science fact. But probably his best known work is the film *2001: A Space Odyssey*, which he adapted from one of his own short stories in collaboration with the producer-director Stanley Kubrick.

Although we are now living in the space age, and indeed the year 2001 is not very far away, science fiction from Lucian to Clarke still remains popular with all ages. This is due to the fact that it appeals to the spirit of adventure that lies within all men. Science fiction will continue to change, but it is certain that the incredible machines, monstrous robots, fantastic journeys, and even the bug-eyed monsters will stay popular for a long, long time.

Is There Life Out There?

One question that is continually being asked with regard to space is 'Is there life out there?' If by 'life' we mean creatures and plants similar to those found on Earth, then the same conditions that exist on our planet must also be present in outer space if life is to be found. In the Solar System, none of the planets contains the vital ingredients – oxygen, water and an even temperature – in the right proportions. Most of the larger planets are too cold. Many of the smaller ones are too hot. Some such as Mercury and the Moon have no atmosphere so they can be ruled out immediately. In examining our Solar System, it would seem that the only planets, apart from our own, that can support life might be Mars and Venus.

Probes to Mars have not yet found any evidence that life exists. And Venus remains rather a mystery for we still know very little about it. It should be borne in mind, however, that even though we could not exist on these planets, other life forms may be able to.

The climatic conditions found on Mars have so far ruled out the possibility of any form of life existing there. In recent years, however, scientists have discovered bacteria, algae, and fungi on Earth in the Dry Valleys of the Antarctic, an area previously thought incapable of supporting any life form. The conditions in this part of the Antarctic are in many ways similar to those found on Mars, so it seems quite feasible that similar life forms may exist there also. They may not be the little green men that many people hope for, but if such micro-organisms did exist on Mars, it would prove that Earth is not the only planet capable of supporting life. As a result, there would be an increased effort to continue the search for more advanced forms of life.

Our Sun is just but one of many millions of stars that abound in the Milky Way galaxy. Many of these stars will have their own 'solar' systems. Unfortunately, such planets would be too small for us to detect. Perhaps one day we will have the capability to visit some of these other worlds. We will then discover once and for all whether there are other living creatures in the galaxy. Whether this discovery will prove to be good or bad remains to be seen.

The Pioneer 10 probe launched on 2 March 1972, carried a gold anodised aluminium plate on which there were engraved diagrams of the Earth's position in space, and drawings of a man and a woman. The man was shown with his hand held up in greeting, in the hope that should any aliens discover the plaque, they would realise that we wish to make contact and that our intentions are friendly.

Most scientists believe that our initial contact with other beings, should they exist, will not be through probes like Pioneer 10, but by means of radio. As early as 1899, scientists were receiving signals from outer space and attributing them to intelligent forms of life. One of the first to receive such signals, was Nikola Tesla. He was convinced that some form of extra terrestrial life was trying to contact Earth. The inventor of the radio, Marconi, also picked up signals from space in 1921.

In 1961, the distinguished astronomer, Dr Otto Struve, set up Project Ozma to monitor Tau Ceti, one of the nearest suns to us likely to have planets like our own. Within two minutes of listening, unmistakable signals were received from the area. Struve was certain he had received a coded message.

In late 1978, American scientists began a five year pro-gramme of listening for extra terrestrial beings. For this project, which has the backing of NASA, they are using the giant radio telescopes at the Jet Propulsion Laboratory in California.

There is only one problem in trying to contact other beings by radio. If such beings are far in advance of us, they may have given up radio as a primitive form of communication several thousand years ago, when men on Earth were just beginning to emerge from their caves.

Journey To The Stars (*Game*)

It may be some time before you get the chance actually to journey to the stars. You can, however, imagine that you are on such a journey with this space-age game.

Copy the number star onto card and cut it out. Push the stub of a pencil through the centre of the number star.

Copy the space ships onto some pieces of card, cut them out, and colour them in. Do the same with the board. Again colour this in with bright colours. (*See over page.*)

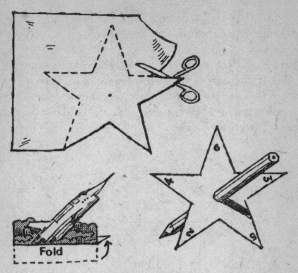

Journey to the stars

When you have completed the board, write the following instructions for players on or near the numbers mentioned:

4. Martian base out of supplies – go back one space.

9. Obtain fuel supplies from Saturn – blast off to star 15.

12. Hit by a meteorite swarm – miss a turn while damage is being repaired.

17. Attacked by space pirates – take evasive action by going back two spaces.

25. Arrive at space station CGX325 1a and rest for two days – miss a turn.

29. Take on nuclear fuel from Pluto base. Ship takes off on schedule so move to star 34.

32. Your ship becomes trapped in gravity pull – move to the black hole.

Black hole

33. Friendly robot-controlled starship transports you across the galaxy at high speed – move three stars.
40. Proxima Centuri.
47. Space storm forces you to take cover – go back to Proxima Centuri.
Black Hole: You are trapped in this black hole until you score a six. When you do, move to space station CGX325 1a and miss one go.

To start the game each player puts his spaceship onto the launch pad. You then take it in turns to spin the number star. The number that is pointing upwards to the stars when the number star comes to rest, is the number of places you can move forward on the board. Each player takes it in turn to do this, and the first one to reach Alpha Centuri is the winner.

To add some extra excitement to the game, you can make it a rule that if a spaceship lands on a space that is already occupied, the one that was there first is blasted out of the skies and has to start again from the launch pad. This should be agreed by all players before the start of the game.

If, by a stroke of misfortune, you are sucked into the black hole, you have to throw a six to get yourself out again. When the six has been thrown, the spaceship can be placed back on the planet Neptune. Better be careful you do not score a two now, or you will be sucked into the black hole once more!

The U.F.O. Mystery

Reported sightings of 'flying saucers' or UFOs (unidentified flying objects), have been common since the dawn of civilisation. Several references to what would today be classed as UFO sightings can be found in the Bible and ancient writings, but possibly the first book to be devoted solely to this subject was *Strange Signes from Heaven*, which was published in 1646.

Eight years before that book was written, James Everett and two friends were sailing a barge along the Muddy River in Massachusetts when an enormous light dived from the sky. The power emanating from the light was so great that the boat was pulled upstream against the tide by an invisible force until, after some twenty minutes or so, the light vanished and the men were able to row to the shore.

In 1873, a large, cigar-shaped object flew at great speed over Bonham in Texas. The following day, what was apparently the same thing whizzed over the parade ground at Fort Scott, Kansas, about 350 miles from Bonham. Once again it swooped low over the ground and flew off at great speed. To this day no-one has found a satisfactory solution as to what that object was.

Nine years later, in the early evening of 17 November 1882, Walter Maunder, an astronomer, was on the roof of London's Greenwich Observatory when he saw 'a great circular disc of greenish light' which moved across the sky 'as smoothly and steadily as the sun, moon, stars, and planets move, but nearly a thousand times as quickly.' He described the object as an elongated ellipse – 'cigar-shaped or like a torpedo' – exactly the same description that was to be applied to many of the UFOs sighted in the twentieth century.

During the summer of 1917, John Boback was walking along a railway track in Pennsylvania, USA, when he heard a swishing sound to his left. Looking round, he saw to his astonishment that an elliptical craft had landed in a field less than a hundred metres from where he stood. A few seconds later, the vessel lifted from the ground and flew off.

Six years later, a flying saucer as large as a modern passenger plane and emitting a bright red light was seen hovering 200 metres above a main road near Indianapolis. Two men, who were later to become university professors, witnessed this event; and a similar vessel was seen by two cattlemen in North Dakota five years later.

The first of the modern sightings took place on 24 June 1947. Kenneth Arnold, an American businessman, was piloting a private plane over a range of snow-capped mountain peaks when he saw a number of bright 'saucer-like things.' It was the first time that the word had been used to describe UFOs. 'Flying saucer' has now become part of our language. But the mystery of what they are and where they come from still remains.

In February 1954, Cedric Allingham was enjoying a quiet country walk when he saw a flying saucer. It landed quite close to him as he was walking near Lossiemouth in Scotland. As he stood there in open-mouthed amazement, wondering whether to stand or run, a door in the strange craft slid open and a young man in a shining metallic suit stepped out.

The stranger stood almost two metres in height and he had brown, short hair. Apart from a very high forehead and a deep tan, this visitor from beyond the stars looked rather like an ordinary human. Using a notebook and pencil, Allingham was able to conduct a conversation with his new-found friend, who had apparently come from Mars.

The amazing thing about the whole episode was that it had been independently witnessed. From a nearby hill, fisherman James Duncan had watched Allingham's meeting and had seen the alien return to his space craft and take off.

Cedric Allingham wrote a book about his unusual experience and then apparently disappeared. Was this, perhaps, just another hoax in the flying saucer saga?

Some people have claimed actually to have been inside a flying saucer. One such person was Dino Kraspedon who, while in Sao Paulo in November 1952, saw several saucers and was eventually given the chance of going into one and to meet the crew. At a later date, the captain of the saucer had long discussions with Kraspedon in which the alien explained how flying saucers were powered, the true nature of energy and matter, and many other scientific subjects. He also stated that in our solar system, the planets of Mercury, Venus, Mars, Uranus, Neptune and Pluto are also inhabited.

Possibly the best known name connected with flying saucers is that of George Adamski, who claimed that on 20 November 1952, when he and some friends were in the Californian Desert looking for space ships (several sightings had been reported in the area), he met and conversed with a man from Venus. On both this and a subsequent occasion, he managed to obtain some good photographs of the space craft. Controversy still rages as to whether the pictures he took are genuine or extremely clever fakes.

Three years after Adamski's encounter with a flying saucer, Elizabeth Klarer was invited inside one of these mysterious craft in South Africa. She was walking on her sister's farm one day in 1955 when she came across the saucer. It was circular with evenly spaced portholes and was standing on three legs. Elizabeth was not frightened, as she had seen the same saucer in flight some eighteen months earlier. Beside the craft was a man-like figure who invited her in to view the craft.

The main cabin of the ship was circular and had two smaller cabins leading off it. A second man showed her the control panels as the craft took to the air. Through a lens in the centre of the main cabin she could see the earth receding beneath her. She was also shown a room in which the occupants grew all their own food. When she asked how the craft worked, she was told 'the propulsion system sets up a magnetic field around the ship, causing it to glow. This is electrical and the changes of colour people report seeing are created by the field differentials surrounding the ship in different light or time speeds.'

According to Elizabeth Klarer, the saucer came from Alpha Centauri, where there is a civilisation far superior to anything yet found on Earth. Apparently, the aliens took an interest in this planet because they are concerned about the way we are fast destroying our own world with pollution and nuclear devices.

Many sightings have been made by people whose jobs ensure that they are trained observers. Police constables Clifford Waycott and Roger Willey could hardly believe their eyes as they drove along a quiet English road in Devon, early one morning in October 1967. Hovering just above them was a bright ball of light. They accelerated after it, but the 'Thing' must have seen them also for it, too, moved away and, even though at times the police car reached ninety miles an hour, they were unable to catch whatever it was.

It was later joined by a cross-shaped light, which was also extremely bright, before the two of them disappeared as mysteriously as they had come.

Soon afterwards some other policemen, in Derbyshire, saw a similar cross-shaped formation of lights in the sky. Many hundreds of similar occurrences were reported between 25 and 27 October that year.

These phenomena 'appeared' during a period when the US Air Force had been carrying out mid-air refuelling exercises, and for a time this was accepted as a reasonable explanation for the sightings – until it was pointed out that the exercises had taken place between 5 p.m. and 9 p.m. – but the lights had been seen between midnight and daybreak!

In 1975, six woodmen were driving home from work at Snowflake, Arizona, USA, when they were stopped by a flying saucer. One of the men, Travis Walton, leapt out of the car to investigate and was promptly knocked to the ground by a flash of light from the craft. As the other men watched in transfixed amazement, the crew got out of the spacecraft and carried their friend inside. Travis was not seen again until five days later, when he suddenly woke up near the same spot. He said that he had spent the time in the company of the alien creatures. 'They were certainly not human,' he said, and described them as being about five feet in height, with human-like features but with a very white skin, dome-shaped forehead and very large eyes.

Towards the end of 1978, came reports that the supersonic airliner Concorde was being shadowed by a UFO. Eye witnesses described it as a huge ball of reddish light that appeared to be keeping a watch on the aircraft as it came in to land at Heathrow Airport. Nothing to explain the light was picked up by the airport radar, so it seems that at the present this is just one more mystery to add to the never-ending list of phenomena that are classed as UFOs.

Some people have put forward the theory that UFOs are not from outer space but from within our own environment, and that they are not mechanical but living things. It is thought that they are, in fact, devils and angels which live in a parallel world to our own. In the most part the people who have advanced this theory state that flying saucers are not therefore of benefit to man, but are out to destroy the world as we know it. Not a very pleasant thought!

When discussing UFOs, the word 'hoax' often creeps into the conversation, and it is true that there have been a number of cases in which the main player was the victim of an elaborate practical joke, or the joker himself.

Some hoaxes, are, of course, organised by those whose only interest is to cash in on the UFO phenomena by getting their names in the papers or being interviewed on television. Many of the sightings of UFOs have, however, been made by responsible and intelligent people.

Official sources are reluctant to disclose what they think

about the subject. When they do release information, it is invariably to prove that such things as flying saucers simply do not exist. On one occasion the British Ministry of Defence conducted detailed investigations of 1631 UFO sightings reported over a six year period. The Ministry said that 750 of the sightings were proved to be nothing more than ordinary aircraft, 203 were accounted for by satellites or space debris, 173 were insufficiently detailed to form any opinion, 170 were definitely stars, 121 were meteor formations, 108 were meteorological balloons, and 106 were simply lights or flares.

After sifting through all the reports of UFOs and eliminating those that have a rational explanation, one is invariably left with quite a large number that cannot be explained in conventional terms. Whether or not these occurrences were caused by beings from outer space remains to be proved, but it does not seem unreasonable to assume that there could be life on other planets capable of such achievements.

Our Earth is only one of the many million planets in our galaxy and there are millions of other galaxies, with as many planets, beyond our own. It is more than likely that life exists or has existed on one or several of these other 'worlds'. If one considers Man's fantastic progress from his first flight to space travel in about sixty years, it is possible that beings from other planets have made similar, or even faster and more advanced, progress. Who can say, therefore, that such people have not discovered high-speed interplanetary travel? Perhaps one day we will know for certain. . . .

Making A Flying Saucer

For a flying saucer you will need a cheese carton, a margarine carton, the top from an aerosol can and some glue.

Glue the top and bottom of the cheese carton together so they will not come apart. On top of this glue the margarine carton. If you find that this does not stick very well, try using some sticky tape instead of glue. On top of the margarine carton glue the aerosol top and your flying saucer is complete. All you now need to do is to paint it. Put an overall coat of silver on the flying saucer, using an aerosol paint obtainable from your local motor accessories shop, and then paint the various details, such as the door and the portholes, with an ordinary paintbrush and poster paint.

Photograph A U.F.O.

A large number of photographs showing flying saucers have been proved to be fakes. Some involved the use of quite complicated photographic techniques, but it is possible to produce realistic-looking pictures without a special knowledge of photography.

One of the simplest ways to fake a picture of a UFO is first to make a flying saucer like the one described on page 95. Take it outside and set the shutter of your camera at a fast speed. Now all you have to do is throw the saucer into the air and take a picture of it. It is as simple as that! You can do it with any round disc-shaped object, but you may have to take several pictures to get the craft at the best angle.

Using the same model saucer, you could string it up between two trees with a length of thin thread. And then just photograph it and you will have a realistic-looking picture.

Some published pictures purporting to be of UFOs are

extremely blurred, and this in many people's minds makes them even more realistic. All you have to do to achieve the same effect is make sure that the object is out of focus when you take the photograph.

To achieve pictures of lights in the sky, try taking a photograph of a torch held behind a sheet. This produces a diffused effect that can easily be mistaken for strange lights. You could perhaps rig up several lights behind a sheet to get an even better picture.

One final point. Only take pictures for the amusement of yourself and your friends. Do not try to pretend that they really are pictures of flying saucers, for experts can readily tell whether or not a photograph is faked. And they have to deal with enough cranks without adding you to their list.

But if you do happen to see a flying saucer, make sure you have got your camera with you. You never know what may develop!

Make An Alien Robot

To make this alien robot you will need first the inner cardboard tube from a roll of kitchen paper or something similar. If you cannot find one, an empty washing up liquid container with the top removed will do just as well. Alternatively, you can make a suitable tube from paper or card. To the top of the tube glue or tape the top from an aerosol can. Paint a face on the front of the aerosol cap and glue pipe cleaners to each side. These can be bent into any shape you like.

Paint the body of your robot and glue buttons onto it to represent the various controls. If you would like to give your robot a pair of arms, you can use two more pipe cleaners, or tubes made of paper, and glue them to each side of the body.

To make your robot move of its own accord, you will need a special motor made from a cotton reel, a circular block of wood about one centimetre thick with a hole through its centre, two matchsticks, a piece of candle about a centimetre thick, and an elastic band. Remove the wick and make a small hole in the centre of the piece of candle. Making this hole is quite a tricky operation, so take your time and be careful how you go about it. Possibly the easiest way to make this hole is to burn through the candle with a hot poker, but please get an adult to do this for you or you may burn yourself.

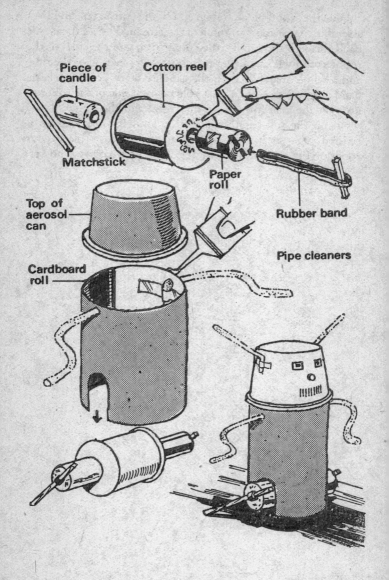

Piece of candle

Cotton reel

Matchstick

Paper roll

Rubber band

Top of aerosol can

Pipe cleaners

Cardboard roll

Glue the wood block to one end of the cotton reel and then assemble the various components as shown. Thread the elastic band through the candle, the cotton reel, and the sides of the robot as shown. Use half a matchstick on one side of the tube and a whole matchstick on the candle side to hold the elastic band in position. Cut an oval hole on each side of the robot to go over the axle formed by the wood and the candle. Now wind up the full-length matchstick until the elastic band is twisted as far as it will possibly go. If you now place your robot on the ground, it will move along under its own power.

Make A Telescope

To make this telescope you will need first two *convex* lenses. These can be salvaged from an old pair of binoculars, or magnifying glasses. The focal length of one of these lenses should be several times that of the other. Thus, if the smaller of the two is 5 centimetres, the focal length of the other should be between 10 and 30 centimetres.

If you do not know the focal length of a lens, you can find out what it is by focusing the sun's rays onto a sheet of card. Move the lens in relation to the card until the rays are concentrated into a tiny pinprick of light. Heat, too, is concentrated at this point, so be careful that you do not set the card on fire.

Now measure the distance from the card to the lens. That distance is the focal length.

The body of the telescope must be as long as the combined focal lengths of the two lenses you are using. If, for example, one lens has a focal length of 5 centimetres and the other is 30 centimetres, your telescope will have to be 35 centimetres long.

Divide this figure by two ($35 \div 2 = 17\frac{1}{2}$), add a few centimetres for overlap, and this will give you the length of each of the two tubes that will make up your telescope. In this example, each tube will therefore be about 20 centimetres long.

Make the tubes out of cartridge paper or thin card. You

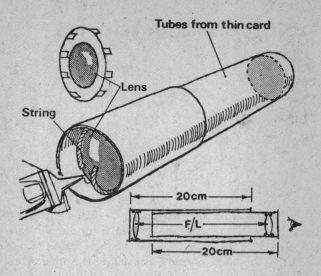

Tubes from thin card

Lens

String

20cm

F/L

20cm

may have to roll it around several times, or use several layers of paper to give the necessary rigidity. One tube should be just wide enough to take the lens with the longer focal length. The second tube takes the other lens and should fit snugly into the first tube.

To hold each lens in place, take some string and glue it around the inside of the tube. When the glue has dried, push the lens into position and then glue another piece of string in front of the lens to hold it in place.

Because the two tubes must fit neatly together, you may find that the small lens is, in fact, too small to fit into the inner tube. This can be overcome by making a ring of cardboard of the correct size to fit into the tube. Glue this to the lens and then glue the ring into position.

Place one tube into the other, look through the smaller one, and adjust the positioning of the two tubes until the object at which you are looking is in focus. Because this telescope produces an inverted image, it is therefore only really suitable for studying the night sky.

How To Make A Star Chart

All astronauts need to have a good working knowledge of astronomy. Part of this knowledge includes the ability to pick out the various constellations in the night sky. This information can be learned from books and by observing the night sky, but the best way is to gain the knowledge in a practical way. One way you can do this is to make your own star chart.

Before you can begin drawing the star chart you must first plot the positions of the stars in the sky. The easiest way to do this is simply to take a piece of clear plastic and hold it up to the sky and then draw, with the aid of a chinagraph (grease) pencil, the positions of all the stars you can see.

To keep the plotter steady whilst you do this, make a simple handle from two pieces of wood. One is about 22 centimetres (9 inches) long and the other should be about 15 centimetres (6 inches). Drill two holes through the top of the shorter piece and two similar holes through the plastic. Two screws are now pushed through the short piece of wood and the plastic and screwed into the longer piece of wood as shown.

You will now find that if you place the end of the long piece of wood against your cheekbone and hold the short piece in your hand the plotter can be held quite steady. If you find the long piece of wood is too long for you to hold the

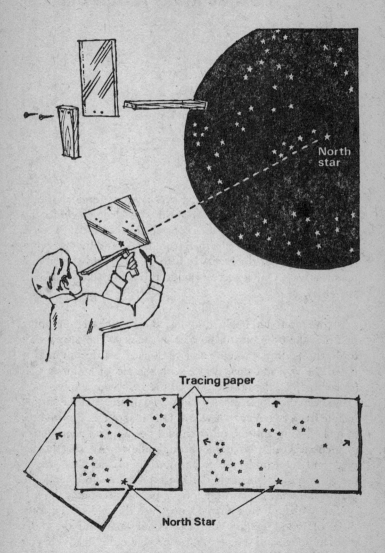

Tracing paper

North Star

How to make a star chart

plotter comfortably, you can always shorten it. To further reduce the strain on your arm and to obtain even more support, you could screw the handle of the plotter onto the end of a broom handle. Rest the other end of the broom handle on the ground and you will find that you can use the plotter quite readily.

Take the plotter out into your garden and look along the long piece of wood up at the night sky. Position yourself so that the north star is placed in the centre of the bottom of the plastic. With the grease pencil, mark the position of the star on the plastic plate. Then continue to mark the positions of all the other stars you can see. When you have finished, draw an upward pointing arrow in the centre of the top of the chart.

Disassemble the plotter and take the plastic sheet indoors. Place a sheet of tracing paper over the plastic and trace all the stars you have noted. To stop the tracing paper moving while you do this, tape it to the plastic.

Now wipe the plastic clean, reassemble the plotter, and you are ready for the next part of the operation. Exactly four hours after your first observation, go outside again and draw the position of the stars on the plastic as you did before. Once again, go indoors and trace this onto a sheet of tracing paper.

Place the second sheet on top of the first and position the two north stars so that one is on top of the other. Now carefully move the second sheet to the right until the stars that appear on both sheets overlap. Tape the two sheets down so they will not move.

Now take a third, larger, sheet of tracing paper and place it over the two smaller pieces. Copy all the star-positions onto the large sheet. You now have a star chart showing all the stars that are visible on a particular night.

This has taken quite a lot of work to prepare so far, but you can still take the process a step further. The chart you have drawn shows only half the stars that may be visible in the night sky. The remaining stars will not be visible until six months later. So, if you would like to make a complete map of all the stars you are likely to see at any time of the year, you will have to make a second chart. This is made in exactly the same way as the first, but the observations must be made six months later, on the same day of the month. When you put the two charts together you will have a complete map of the night sky as seen from the part of the world in which you live.

Looking At The Stars

Although it is great fun making the star chart described on page 103, it does take quite a bit of work. And because you have to wait six months before the whole chart is complete, it takes rather a lot of time before you can see any really useful results. For those who cannot wait, here is an even easier way of learning the various constellations.

First copy the two halves of the star chart shown on the following pages onto a sheet of tracing paper. Draw the two halves fitted together so they make three quarters of a circle as shown. Cut out the shape together with a small flap along one edge and then bend it round into a cone shape with the stars on the inside. Glue the flap to hold the cone in shape.

If you live in the southern hemisphere you will have to

make a similar chart showing all the stars that can be seen in your part of the world. Do not forget to leave a gap so you can form it into a cone.

Take this paper cone out into the garden at night and you can use it to pick out the principal constellations. Point the tip of the cone towards the north star and then revolve it until the Plough on the cone is more or less lined up with the Plough constellation.

The Plough is the easiest constellation to spot in the northern hemisphere. It consists of a group of seven stars resembling the shape of a saucepan (or a plough if you have sufficient imagination). Most of them are very bright, with the exception of the one in the middle of the group, which is sometimes difficult to see.

Once the cone is in position you can use it to find out the names and positions of all the other constellations. You may, of course, need a torch to do this properly.

The only disadvantages of using this method is that the cone is rather small and there is a risk that it will get torn easily. If you do not fancy the idea of making a new cone each time the old one is worn out, you could try the following.

You will need a transparent umbrella. Alternatively, you could make one of your own by stretching some polythene sheeting over the frame of an old umbrella. Now, using the cone chart and a light coloured chinagraph pencil or some white paint, copy the positions of the constellations onto the inner surface of the umbrella. Do this as carefully as you can. It does not matter if you are not spot on with this drawing, but the better and more accurately you do it, the more effective will it be in use. The umbrella is used in exactly the same fashion as the paper cone described above. Use a torch to illuminate the interior of the umbrella if need be.

Scorpion

Scales

Hercules

Northern crown

Herdsman

Virgin

Water serpent

Little bear

Lion

Great bear

North star here

Crab

Little dog

Twins

Great dog

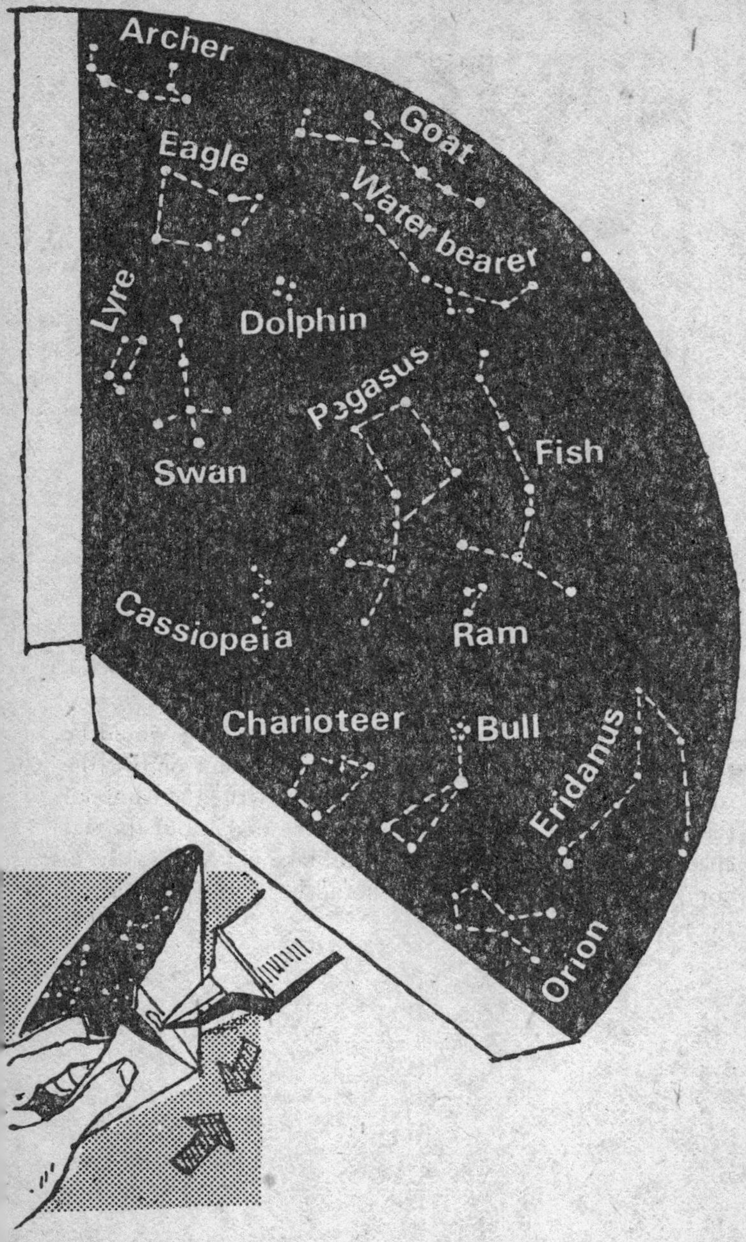
Archer
Goat
Eagle
Water bearer
Lyre
Dolphin
Pegasus
Fish
Swan
Cassiopeia
Ram
Charioteer
Bull
Eridanus
Orion

Looking at the stars

Another way of accomplishing the same thing would be to take the clear umbrella out and simply paint onto it the stars that you can see through it. You can write the names of the constellations in afterwards. Like the making of the star chart described on page 103, this will take you six months to complete, by which time you should be quite an expert on the night sky.

Become A Robot

It is more than likely that robots will be used in the future to control many of the functions within a spacecraft, and perhaps act as servants to the men who are exploring space. To make such a computerised robot requires considerable technical expertise, a scientific background, and an expert knowledge of computers. For you to make a robot the task is a great deal simpler – all you need is two cardboard boxes, a large one and a small one.

The large box should be big enough to go completely over your body. The small box should be big enough to fit over your head. You should be able to get two suitable boxes from your local supermarket.

The bottom of both boxes should be open. In the top of the large box, make a hole big enough to put your head through. Make some small holes in one side of the small box. If you now put the large box over your body, put your head through the hole, and then put the small box over your head, you will see that you are beginning to look something like a real robot.

You can move around quite easily just by walking normally, but no-one will be able to see your feet as they will be hidden inside the large box. As the two boxes are not connected together in any way, you will also find it very easy to move your head around to see where you are going (the holes you made in the side of the small box will enable you to do this).

Become a robot

Your robot can be made to look more impressive by painting it. You could also stick some buttons or discs of card onto the front and sides to represent the controls. If you would like to give your robot arms, simply make a hole in each side, or in the front, of the large box through which you can put your arms. To make these arms look more like a robot's arms, ask your mother for an old pair of tights or stockings. Fix one stocking leg into each of the armholes you have just made. You then put your arms into the stockings just as you would when putting them into the sleeves of a jumper. In fact, if you cannot get any suitable tights or stockings, the sleeves of an old jumper would do just as well.

Cut some discs of various sizes from card, and make holes in their centres, sufficiently large so you can push them onto your arms to make them look more mechanical.

As an alternative to giving your robot arms, you could equip it with simple wooden struts or even weapons. The struts would be simply lengths of wood pushed through holes in the front of the large box. You will be able to move these up and down from inside the box. Weapons could be carved out of wood or made of cardboard glued over wooden struts. These would be operated from inside the box in the same way as the straightforward struts.

Space Dictionary

AIR LOCK—A chamber attached to the door of a spacecraft that ensures the artificial atmosphere inside the craft does not escape when an astronaut wishes to exit or enter.

APOGEE—The point on the orbit of a craft or a satellite when it is furthest from Earth.

ALSEPS—Apollo Lunar Surface Experimental Packages – a group term to cover the various scientific experiments set up on the Moon by the Apollo astronauts.

ASTRONAUT—The word used in the Western world to denote a space traveller. Strictly speaking, the word means 'star traveller'.

ASTRONAUTICS—The science of space travel and exploration.

ATMOSPHERE—The layer of air surrounding Earth. The thickness of the layer varies and the higher the altitude, the less the density of air.

CHICKEN SWITCH—A switch in the capsules of American spacecraft by use of which an astronaut can escape from the craft and abort the mission.

COSMONAUT—Term used by the Russians to denote a spaceman. The word means 'space traveller'.

ESCAPE VELOCITY—The speed a body must reach to escape from a planet's gravitational pull. To launch a craft from Earth requires a speed of more than 17,000 miles an hour.

EYEBALLS IN—Slang term used by American astronauts to describe the G-force that operates on them as they are launched out of the Earth's atmosphere.

EYEBALLS OUT—Used by astronauts to describe the force that occurs as a craft re-enters the Earth's atmosphere.

EVA—Extra Vehicular Activity – or in more conventional terms, any activity outside the spacecraft.

FLOATATION COLLAR—A rubber ring put around American spacecraft when they splashdown in the sea to help keep them afloat. (Russian craft come down on land.)

G-FORCE—A measurement of acceleration in relation to the Earth's gravitational pull. The acceleration at which an object falls to the ground is designated 1G. An astronaut being launched into space has to withstand a force of about 10G.

GEMINI—American spacecraft designed to carry two astronauts. The name means 'the twins'.

GEOSTATIONARY ORBIT—An orbit in which the period of orbit exactly matches the speed of the planet's rotation. For Earth this orbit is achieved at a height of 22,300 miles, with the satellite travelling at 6,900 miles an hour. If a satellite is put into orbit over the equator, in the same direction as the Earth's rotation, it appears to be stationary. Such satellites are used for global telecommunications and weather observations.

HEAT SHIELD—A protective layer on space capsules that prevents the capsule and its occupants from burning up when it re-enters the Earth's atmosphere.

LUNAR ORBITAL RENDEZVOUS—The technique using a Command Module, Service Module, and Lunar Excursion Module, utilised by the Americans during the Apollo programme.

LUNAR ROVING VEHICLE—Moon buggy used by American astronauts to explore the lunar surface. Ten were built and three were used on the moon. (See page 45.)

LUNOKHOD—The Russian automatic lunar roving vehicle, the first wheeled vehicle to travel on the Moon.

NASA—National Aeronautics and Space Administration, the organisation set up on 29 July 1958, to administer America's civil space programme.

ORBITAL VELOCITY—The speed required to keep a body in orbit. This speed varies according to the height of the orbit. The higher the orbit the lower the speed required to keep the craft in position.

PERIGEE—The point in a satellite's orbit when it is nearest to Earth.

PLiSS—Personal Life Support Systems – the term used to describe the backpack carried by lunar astronauts. These packs supply oxygen for breathing and for pressurising the spacesuit. They also supply water to cool the astronaut's body, by means of an undergarment of tubes that carry it around his body. Although the PLiSS is heavy on Earth, it seems much lighter on the Moon because there lunar gravity is only one sixth that of Earth.

RETRO-ROCKET—Rockets used to slow down a spacecraft. To do this, the rockets are fired in the direction that the craft is travelling.

SYNCHRONOUS ORBIT—Same as Geostationary Orbit.

TELEMETRY—The measurement, recording, and transmission of data by a remote sensor or a space probe.

VOSKHOD—Russian spacecraft capable of carrying up to three men. In design it was more or less the same as its predecessor the Vostok but larger. The first manned test flight took place in October 1964.

ZERO-G—A condition of no gravity when weightlessness occurs.

Make A Space Mobile

This space mobile will make a great decoration for an astronaut's bedroom. To make it you will need one piece of copper wire about 22 centimetres (9 inches) long and four pieces about 15 centimetres (six inches) long. Get an adult to cut the wire into the correct lengths. The shop where you buy the wire may do this for you. At the same time, ask the person concerned to bend each end of each piece of wire over to provide hooks on which you can hang the various suspended designs.

Copy some pictures of spaceships from books or magazines onto card and paint them. Make a small hole in the top of each spaceship. Tie some cotton through the holes and you are ready to hang the ships from the wires.

The next stage in making the space mobile is not difficult, but it does require some patience. Tie a spaceship to each end of two of the shorter wires, and one spaceship to one end of the other two short wires. To the opposite end of the wires that have only one spacecraft tie a length of cotton. Tie the other end of this cotton to the centre of one of the wires that support two ships. Move the cotton along the wire until the two lower ships are perfectly balanced. This may take some time.

When you have got the wire balanced, put some glue around the knot in the cotton to hold it in position.

Do exactly the same with the other two wires, again balancing the two-ship wire beneath the one-ship wire.

Now take the long wire and tie a length of cotton to each end of it. The lower end of each of these threads has now to

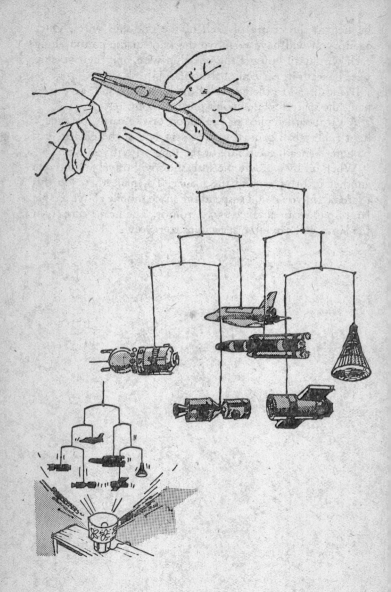

be tied to the centre of each of the one-ship wires. Once again, you will have to move the knot in the cotton along each wire until you get the one-ship wire, and the two-ship wire beneath it, perfectly balanced.

Tie a thread to the centre of the long wire and use this to hang the space mobile up in your bedroom.

A cardboard replica of the moon or the earth, or even a light rubber ball painted to represent one of the planets, can be hung beneath the centre of the long wire if you wish.

When hit by a breeze the spaceships will travel around one another in orbit around the planet. To make them do this more often, you could suspend the space mobile above a table lamp, but a safe distance away from it. The heat rising from the lamp will cause the spaceships to revolve.

Mysteries In Space

Since the beginning of time space has proved to be a source of continual wonderment and mystery to Man. Gradually as knowledge increased men began to learn how to unravel the mysteries of the heavens above. Solutions were found but were often proved to be inaccurate as more and more was discovered about the amazing Universe, of which our planet is such an infinitesimal part. Down through the centuries astronomers have made remarkable discoveries, many of which clashed with existing theories so violently that the latter had to undergo radical change. In recent years, just as man was beginning to venture into space on his own and thought that he had a reasonable understanding of this strange environment, even more amazing discoveries have been made. Many of these discoveries have come about due to the use of the radio telescope. In many cases the discoveries have been so astonishing and unexpected that they have even the scientists baffled as to their true nature.

In 1962, the whole concept of the nature of the Universe was questioned when quasars were first discovered. Quasars, or quasi-stellar objects, appeared at first to be ordinary stars. But when the scientists investigated them further, they discovered that these strange objects were even farther from Earth than any other known objects. And yet in spite of their extreme distance, they are amazingly bright.

This brightness has posed problems for the scientists, for it has also been proved that quasars are very small. To be as bright as they are, they must be emitting vast amounts of energy – far more than would normally be possible for objects of their size. To add to the confusion, some scientists have suggested that quasars are not so far away from Earth as we once thought. Controversy still rages as to their exact nature, but they are being investigated thoroughly so perhaps one day we will know the answers to the various problems that these strange objects generate.

The search for quasars led to the discovery of another mystery of space – the pulsar, or pulsating star. The first pulsar was discovered by Anthony Hewish at Cambridge University in 1967. He and his colleagues detected radio waves emanating from outer space that were completely unlike anything received previously. One of the things that astonished the scientists at the time was that the radio signals were being transmitted regularly, once every $1\frac{1}{2}$ seconds.

Since that time many other pulsars, pulsating at different rates, have been found, but exactly what is causing the pulsating signal is not known. At first it was thought that the signals were coming from other life forms because they were so regular, but it is now realised that they are of a natural origin. It could be that the bodies emitting the signals are revolving, and that only one portion of the star's surface is emitting the signal. In this way it could be operating in a similar fashion of the light of a lighthouse which one sees at regular intervals as the light revolves. Another possible explanation is that the body is expanding or contracting at a regular rate and with every change in state energy is emitted. This release of energy is picked up as a radio signal by the radio telescopes on Earth.

It is thought that both quasars and pulsars are very small, even though they emit such powerful signals. This may be due to the fact that their density is remarkably high. It may be that they have a connection with another mystery of space – the neutron star. Before the discovery of quasars and pulsars, scientists had put forward the theory that the Universe could contain objects called neutron stars. These were small bodies with a very strong gravitational field. The body itself was created from the central core of a star when the star had exploded. It was reasoned, however, that this core would be so small that it would never be discovered. Quasars and pulsars fulfil the various requisites laid down within these theories and so it would seem that neutron stars, at one time merely a theoretical possibility, do in fact exist.

Because these small objects have such a great gravitational pull, it is thought that this could become so strong that not even light could escape from the pull of the body. If this happened the object would become invisible. John Wheeler, an American physicist, termed these invisible objects 'black holes'. It has been predicted that anything passing close to a black hole will be pulled into its gravitational field and will itself disappear.

In recent years space probes have detected the presence of mysterious X-rays in space. It is thought that these X-rays may denote the presence of these enigmatic black holes. If such objects do exist, they could prove extremely dangerous to the unwary space traveller of the future. The captain of a space vehicle could easily find his craft being sucked into a black hole and he, his crew, and his craft would never be seen again!

Future discoveries may help the space traveller to avoid such traps, for it is certain that the discoveries made so far are only a few of the mysteries that abound in the Universe.

The mysteries of space are so weird and wonderful that at present many of them deny rational explanation. Only a few short years ago these phenomena were part of the world of science fiction. It is therefore quite feasible that much of the science fiction of today will be the science fiction of tomorrow. One such wonder, now being seriously discussed by scientists, is that of time warps. It is thought that if they exist, these could be some form of black hole. A spaceship would enter this void, and suddenly be transported hundreds of light years away from its previous position. In this the warp would act rather like a doorway from one part of the universe to another. If time warps exist, they could prove invaluable to the star traveller of the future. Whether or not a spaceship could survive such a journey and perhaps return to our own galaxy by the same route remains to be seen.

And what will the space traveller find when he goes through the time warp? Will it perhaps be like going through a mirror to discover a galaxy identical to our own but with everything in reverse? Is there perhaps another Earth similar in every way to our own? Perhaps this dual world will be peopled with doubles of everyone living on our own planet. When the space crew land they could easily meet their own double face to face. Perhaps it is even possible that the same events that occur on our Earth would also occur at the same time on this dual world. If this were the case, the astronauts would not be able to meet their doubles, for at the same time they would have travelled in the opposite direction to land on our Earth!

Such possibilities appear to be nothing but fantasy. But who knows? When considering the mysteries of the Universe fantasy and fact seem to weave themselves together and it is difficult to determine where one ends and the other begins. Even scientists have been forced to admit that parallel worlds, where everything is a duplicate of things found on another planet, are a mathematical possibility. Perhaps one day we will know for certain.

Of one thing there is no doubt – that although the Heavens have been studied since the dawn of time, we have only just started our adventure into the mysteries of space. Our generation is on the verge of much greater discoveries and more perplexing mysteries than we can ever conceive of, even in our wildest dreams.

Will This Be The End?

Science fiction writers and several religious sects have often predicted the end of Earth. But so far it has not happened.

It is, in fact, certain that the end of the Earth will not happen in our lifetime, or that of our children, or even their children's children. So there seems little to worry about. If the end of the world should occur in the near future it will come as a result of man's inhumanity to his fellow man or the cumulative effects of continual pollution of the globe and its atmosphere.

Many theories have been advanced as to how the world will end naturally. One possible way is that the Sun could stop providing us with the light and heat we need for our continued existence. If this happened, our world would very quickly become a dead planet rather like the Moon. As the temperatures begin to drop people will be forced to live in underground cities but even this would not save them from their ultimate fate.

This is one eventuality that need not worry us unduly, for experts have calculated that the Sun will continue providing us with its life-giving energy for at least another 5000 million years.

Others have suggested that we are moving closer to the Sun and that we shall eventually be scorched off the face of the Earth. This, if it happened, would be such a gradual process that all life will have ceased long before Earth actually collided with the Sun. Man would have plenty of warning so he could easily prepare for the colonisation of other planets in sufficient time. Again, should this unlikely event occur, it will not happen in the foreseeable future so we have nothing to worry about.

Another theory is that the end of the world will come about when the Universe stops expanding and all matter begins moving inwards. At some stage in this process the whole system will break down and Earth, the planets, and the rest of the bodies in the galaxy would exist no more. This event is so many million of years away that it is more than likely that man will have ceased to exist through natural evolution rather than by any cataclismic means.

All of these possibilities are so unlikely and so remote they need not concern the present generation or indeed any future generation. The events are so far distant that Man may not even exist when they do occur. He may have evolved into something completely unlike the form he takes today, or other more dominant life forms may rule the Earth. If men do still exist and they have not obliterated the human race through warfare or negligence, then civilisation should have advanced to such a degree that well before the end people will have travelled to the stars and colonised worlds well outside our present system. All that men will see of the end of Earth will be a flash of light, like a brilliant exploding star, in the sky of their new world.